# Taking the Quantum Leap to Happiness

by
Dennis R. Zinner, D.C., M.S.

Robert D. Reed Publishers • Bandon, OR

**Robert D. Reed Publishers**
P.O. Box 1992
Bandon, OR 97411
Phone: 650-994-6570 • Fax: -6579
E-mail: 4bobreed@msn.com
web site: www.rdrpublishers.com


Typesetter: **Barbara Kruger**
Cover Designer: **Grant Prescott**


ISBN 1-931741-43-3

Library of Congress Control Number 2004092023


Manufactured, typeset and printed in the United States of America

**Dedicated to**

My Grandkids

Andrea, Jeffery, Ashley, Whitney, Shay, and Taurean

# Acknowledgments

This book is not the brain child of one person. It is an accumulation of knowledge dating back to the ancient teachers, philosophers and sages continuing to today's brilliant science philosophers who have had the courage to step beyond the realms of "normal science." I thank them all for braving the fight to return man and woman to place of wholeness and not just an accumulation of atoms.

I would also like to thank my wife, Marilyn, for her patience with me as I wrote this book and especially for choosing me as the one she wanted to walk arm-in-arm with through this lifetime.

I also want to thank Jessica Bryan who did the painstaking job of editing.

# Contents

# Freedom

Life is abundance
So we dig and plow
Waiting for the harvest
Freedom is now.

Life is thoughts
Future and past
Live for the moment
Freedom will last.

Life is activity
Life is rest.
Seeing the contrast,
Freedom is no test.

Life is beyond
A grain of sand
Look to its center
Freedom is at hand.

Freedom is close
Freedom is near
Look inside
Freedom is here.

Freedom is life
Freedom is dear
Open up
Freedom is everywhere

Freedom is love
Freedom won't cease
Find the center
Freedom is peace.

# Author's Note

Most of humanity is ruled and confined by seemingly never-ending circles. Like rats caught in a maze, we search endlessly for liberation from proscribed standards of behavior and experiences forced on us by others: our schools, our political institutions, our laws, the linear teachings of science, our churches, and the unconscious family patterns that are passed down from generation to generation. We play the game without knowing we are playing it.

However, I believe freedom from these never-ending circles is possible. It is possible to break the chains that bind us if we hold unto an understanding and vision of personal freedom.

Within the following pages I will discuss how never-ending circles are formed and the criteria for their existence. These circles are built one upon the other, giving the appearance of chaotic structure, but when broken down to their parts they become palatable. I will show how we pretend that these circles run our lives and that by not giving the circles, and therefore the inherent games of each circle, power by pretending they are real, we can destroy their illusionary power.

Why is this important? It is not important for the person who is content with life. It is only important for the person who wants to grow and especially those who want to reach for unlimited freedom. This book offers a way to change our thought process and capture the ultimate of rewards: becoming unencumbered by life as we now know it.

Hopefully this book will show that no matter what is happening around us, it is an expression of God's love. This love is the sole motivating energy for everything that happens on this planet.

I am thankful that I was allowed to go through the process of writing this book. It changed my life and helped me let go of the many petty expectations and judgments that clouded my perception of what was right action for me.

One of the purposes of this book is to show how to enjoy yourself amidst the tedious muck and mire of daily life. This is accomplished by moving to a place of non-judgment of yourself and others. In this place where everyone is entitled to be who they wish to be, we find that only action through love exists. If we do not judge and, in fact, understand the basis of why we are here, we find that things are the way they are in our lives only because we choose them to be that way. And, yes, we can change anything in our lives by opting for a change and then taking the right action necessary to create that change.

Life is not complicated unless we choose it to be. Our freedom of choice is a facet of our being that is seldom used. We have been tricked into believing that once we make a choice it is permanent. You will see, as I have seen, that freedom of choice is our greatest gift.

I hope you will come to know that every action taken allows us the opportunity to express love. I see now that when I was in sales I used it as an avenue to express love, not strictly as a way to earn money. Also this book was written not as a medium to impart knowledge, but as a way for me to express love. All of us opt for situations that will teach us openness and how to love more fully, because love is all there is: it is the one thing that is with us no matter where we are, what we are doing, or who we are with. Many of us believe that we are in a school on this planet and we may be, not to acquire knowledge per se, but to learn to express love in as many ways as possible.

This book is, I realize, a personal journey for me, but I offer my experiences with love to hopefully lighten your path and to help you see how God is in everything, everybody, and every action.

# Chapter 1

## Introduction

I believe many revelations and miracles happen when we have reached a point when our course of action no longer makes any sense. I was at this place when the idea of this book came to me. Not much made sense, every avenue and activity reeked of irrelevance. I saw myself working to earn enough money so I could afford to continue to work. I exercised and ate properly so I could be healthy enough to go to work to earn enough money to afford to stay healthy. Mine was a world of never-ending circles.

Many of us have been raised with a rigidly disciplined work ethic. We are taught that if we work many hours a day and push ourselves in order to get ahead, we can then be released from these never-ending circles. Once out of these ruts we can be truly free to do whatever we would like whenever we like. We define the term for this state of being in this society as retirement. How often do we hear someone say that they would like to retire at the age of thirty? Or a person who can hardly wait until he can retire at sixty-five? Are they not saying that they have a desire to be freed from their perception of the never-ending circle? The former envisions getting out of the circle early in life, while the latter wants to get out because he is tired of the same old routines.

It appears that human nature requires that we put a proverbial carrot out in front of us to get us moving in some predestined direction—the carrot could be some new understanding, accomplishment, or object to own. These carrots are either to make our ride in the circle more comfortable, expand our circle to make it more complex and challenging, or to move us out of one circle and into another.

I have spent the majority of my adult life in sales, and as such, I have lived a very goal-oriented existence. Almost always when I reached a goal, I found myself becoming more unsatisfied. This dissatisfaction created a great dichotomy in my life: I had achieved what I wanted to achieve, but it was not what I really wanted. This created utter confusion and, as might be suspected, my business would fall off dramatically or some other phenomenon would come into my life to create chaos. The answer to this dilemma, which was reiterated by all the sales gurus who taught sales training techniques, was to find another goal and take off again. It became apparent after many years of striving for bigger and greater material achievements that I was acquiring many things but really was not getting to a place of fulfillment. No matter what I did, I was still housed snugly within my never-ending circles. To sit back and enjoy my success seemed impossible.

We are a goal-oriented society and use goal-setting methods in many aspects of our lives regardless of our occupation. In a country which declares that its sole motivating force is financial profit, it seems rather obvious that it must make profits by keeping people within tightly confined materialistic circles. Profits came to the companies I worked for when they kept me moving toward my personal materialistic goal as well as the company's financial goals. Profits also came to the writers and teachers who preached that if I followed the rules of the circle, someday I, too, would reach financial freedom and would be able to leave my circle and have "the good life."

Yes, it does appear to be a rat race, but does the biggest rat win? Does the fittest one, as Darwin would say, survive? It does not really matter, because without a desire to leave the maze, the race just continues.

There may be some truth to the statement that the meek shall inherit the earth. The state of meekness can only exist in the person who has gained the realization of his lack of importance. He or she no longer needs to prove something to his or her father, mother, brother, sister, neighbor, friend, or self. The meek person neither forces himself or herself nor their ideas upon other people. They observe the events at hand waiting for the right time for action. The only rat who can truly win the race is the one who becomes a mouse.

I am not criticizing the action of running in the pack by participating in these circular races; in many regards it is extremely important. Running with the pack teaches us how to play and what the rules are (and for some of us, motivates us to look elsewhere for personal satisfaction). If everyone creates their own rules for the race, we will experience chaos. Therefore, to avoid chaos, the setting of the rules is the primary responsibility of a society; these rules are set out by both custom and political structure, and within those structures there are rewards for playing within the rules and punishments for not.

To continue this gross analogy of the rat, we need to create a maze to make the race more interesting. The walls of the maze are comprised of society's rules and laws and were initially put in place by the Constitution of the United States. However, if we used just these walls the participants with special interests would not be able to advance their causes and the rich could not get richer nor the poor get poorer. So, of necessity we have an important arm of society composed of our political governing bodies (local, state, and federal lawmakers).

We have been taught that in a republic the governing bodies represent all the people, but in reality, often when a law is brought before Congress it is to help one section of the population to the detriment of another. Rules and laws are passed to alter the maze, thereby making it more compatible with the wishes of one group.

This brings into play another arm of society, the Supreme Court and its allied inferior courts. Their purpose in this society is to make sure that the walls of the maze provided by the Constitution remain intact and empowered. However, it appears too often that the interpretations of the Constitution handed down by the courts are prejudiced toward their self-serving special interests. We know this to be true because decisions by the Supreme Court are seldom unanimous nor do they represent a general consensus of society. The fact that the judges are nominated for their positions by the political party in power at the time and are lobbied for favorable decisions also suggests a hidden agenda. Yet, almost every decision that the Court makes will in some way alter the rules of our society or the walls of our maze. The point to this political tirade is that many of our never-ending circles are controlled by powerful people with seemingly selfish interests.

An important aspect in evaluating my never-ending circles was to see who gained something by having me in a particular role. In my case, I was controlled by my parents, my spouse, my kids, my boss at work, and the list goes on. Once these controlling factors are identified, it is easy to see when and why I gave up my power of decision to these people. Maybe we cannot see the exact maze in the beginning, but it is relatively easy to see the rewards and punishments these people offer by playing or not playing within their rules.

One of the key identifying phrases, which I will discuss in length later is the "if-then" logic. If you do this for me, then I will give you such and such. How do we get sucked into this? One reason is that we are trained to respond to this game at a very early age. Let's continue with our maze analogy and I will attempt to elucidate this concept.

Once the maze has been created, we need to train the participants. One of the best approaches is through "operant behavioral mechanisms" (behavior that is modified by a system of rewards and punishments), which was discovered by B. J. Skinner, the noted psychologist, in his work with rats. Behavior is taught by another arm of society, the educational system, which is designed to teach the rules of society—how to follow the walls in the maze and how to motivate the novice into wanting to achieve the rewards offered by society's structure, i.e., ring a school bell and hope the students, like Pavlov's dogs, will salivate for a grade of A.

The educational system in this country is an interestingly designed program. It would be reasonable to assume that the more education a person has, the more rewards he or she receives from society. However, it is difficult to find a correlation between the wealthiest people and the highly educated. What we do see very often is the more education a person has, the better they are at staying in the maze. The rules that a Ph.D. learns in relation to their educational process are much more strict than that of a fifth grader. This makes the actions of a highly-educated person more predictable, and because they know the rules, they are usually found in very secure corporate positions. So in theory, we find a relationship between education and job security.

I went through engineering school to get a good job, to have job security. What a strange concept that is, job security. Anyone who has ever been laid-off or fired knows that there is no such thing—security can only come from within and is only achieved by broadening one's scope of reality. The more I read the great philosophers such as Emerson, Thoreau, Plato, Gurdjieff, and Rand, the easier it was for me to see the circle in which I was trapped. Reading philosophers such as these and understanding their thinking processes can help throw open the doors that confine us. A philosopher's job is to examine the walls and the rules of our mazes and point out the fallacies of false walls which are perceived as real, but may not be. Philosophy allows us the opportunity to alter our perceptions so we may see things differently.

It seems a paradox that while philosophy is an important part of academia, it is relegated only to the higher educational arenas, and even there the philosophy departments are under-funded and considered by many to be a course in trivial pursuit. After all, what kind of a job can you get with a Bachelor's Degree in philosophy?

Instead the educational system has hung its hat on the part of life that can be defined by science. It does not teach science as a philosophy, but as a fact, as if science defines reality without any question. As we look at our newly-defined maze from a scientific approach, we can see why this method is taught. It is easy to understand because there is a beginning, an end, and definite paths to walk. Science, as it is currently taught, requires that life be a linear progression and that everything be defined to differentiate it from everything else.

Science is different from the philosophy of metaphysics, which allows us to give meaning to chaos or to the concept that the beginning point and the end point may be the same. While science states that a force is required to move us from point A to point B, metaphysics may say that the best way to get to point B is by not doing anything except change our thought processes. What would science and our educational system be like if they taught that point A and point B may be the same point, only viewed from a different reference perspective? What if they taught that "not-doing" was as valid an approach as "doing"? What would happen to our society if the educational system taught contemplation principles along with computation principles?

When students enter one of society's never-ending circles, given the education of today, they must pretend that it is their circle and accept it as linear. When in reality it is a common sphere with many paths and interactions. It is non-linear (later in this discussion we will change from circles to boxes to add some spice to this logic). Within these spheres, we find myriad circles including financial, political, relationship, sexual, and religious aspects each intertwining amidst the very nature of the individual.

What happens to the novice who is stuffed into a Newtonian circle of action-reaction when he or she does not have an aptitude for linear thinking? Do they have to flunk out of school and be one of society's "failures"? Or is it possible for them to eke out their own way? We will discuss in later chapters how having a non-linear aptitude increases the chances of becoming one of society's artists or geniuses. The person who can balance non-linearity with linear thinking is more apt to derive new methodologies and philosophies and have the capability to put these ideas into either words or actions in a logical, understandable way. In the next chapter, I refer to these people as "quantum thinkers."

We seem to have entered a new age of metaphysical philosophy: Quantum Mechanics is now being applied to more than electrons, and Chaos Theory is advocating universal (metaphysical) patterns (I will discuss these concepts in a later chapter). The educational system must start incorporating more metaphysical philosophy into their curriculum or fall far behind in satisfying society's needs. It will need to concentrate on vertical growth as well as horizontal growth and through this process turn our society into one made up of well-rounded, open individuals unafraid to question the structure of the maze as handed down from generation to generation.

It is difficult to question one's actions in relation to a never-ending circle without having the questions spill over to other parts of one's life. Therefore, the parts of my life that I thought were sane and appropriate also came under scrutiny. In particular, questions arose concerning religious issues and God. I grew up as a Baptist, with God sitting on a throne in heaven ready to nail anyone who stepped out of line. I must admit I had a problem with that model because Jesus contradicted it when He said God was love. But there were other things I could not understand, like why would such a powerful God create a planet and fill it with disease, poverty, and overcrowded conditions? Why would God create a paradise, but not allow everyone to live in peace, joy, and love?

These and many more questions were answered for me by just understanding to a small degree that everything does happen as a direct result of God's love for us, and at the same time, by the love in all who we meet.

# Chapter 2
## My Dream

It is relatively easy to look back on the changes in my life and analytically describe what happened, especially considering the theories and vocabulary regarding co-dependency, addiction, and abuse. So I can look back and remember myself trapped in never-ending circles and discuss my experiences as if it were a game in which I was but a pawn. These life changes appeared with much more force than can be remembered, usually causing states of depression or total apathy, which are easy states to forget since they cause us to check out of reality while we are experiencing them.

I met my previous life traumas primarily with desperation. I remember crying many times, "Why, my God, have you forsaken me?" After all, wasn't it someone else's fault that I experienced pain in my life, and who better to blame than God since He had control of my life. I was a good person, I thought, and didn't deserve to be on His hit list. It is hard to think back to these experiences at this point in my life without shaking my head in embarrassment, but all those times helped me build my dream.

My life had fallen apart again, because I had just been laid off from my job and my marriage was crumbling like a stale cookie, but for some reason this life crisis was different; I felt at peace during the process. I had given up control—basically I had just thrown up my hands and given up. I was not even concerned that the inevitable chaos, which generally accompanies a life crisis, was going to sneak up from behind me again like it had so many times before and clobber me on the back of my head, sending me to never-never land for weeks or months. I remember questioning myself as to why I felt so calm and concluded that I must have finally learned that nothing is as bad as it seems. If that conclusion was right, it probably also meant that all the previous trauma that I put myself through finally had some value and I was learning to cope with my life traumas. Of course, if the conclusion was wrong, it meant I had finally gone over the edge into psychosis and the white-coated men with the net would soon be knocking at my door.

Whatever it was, I knew that I felt good and at the time I was grateful for that feeling.

I was very thankful that I had learned how to meditate eight years earlier. My meditations had always been cyclic: sometimes they would be wonderful and other times I had trouble even shutting my eyes. But through all the cycles, I persisted to meditate in one form or another. I am not sure if it was all the confusion around me or something else, but my meditations were again a very wonderful part of my life.

In the way that things usually seem to happen, my wife and son had left on a little vacation and I was alone. The peace and quiet was wonderful. One particular night, I was deep in meditation mentally doing a healing ritual with people that come into my mind. It is a wonderful ritual where I make my mind go blank and then ask people who need healing to come to me. When they appear, I wrap them in a beautiful cocoon of healing light and then send them on their way to do their own self-healing. So, on this particular night I was busy doing this meditation when all of a sudden a stranger appeared encased in a beautiful light. I had the feeling he was a very advanced soul. I remember asking myself, "Who am I to give light to him?" when the energy switched and I was receiving light from him. My mind went totally blank, except for the light. I remember feeling how beautifully warm it was as it encompassed my body. There were brilliant colors, so alive the sparkles literally danced together.

As if drawn by a huge magnet, I went further into the light. The further I went, the more non-existent I became, and yet at the same time I became existent with everyone and everything. I understood that we are all God and that separation from God exists only because we choose to be separate. We are only playing a game of hide and seek where God is always "it."

When I came back into awareness of my body, I noticed that I was quite upset and angry. When I observed those feelings, I started to laugh at myself. I was angry because my game had been discovered: the game of pretending I was my ego, of pretending not to love, of pretending not to have abundance, of pretending not to be happy, and of pretending not to be God. The worst part was that I had caught myself.

This experience had the effect of opening my mind to more things because no matter what I read or observed, I was now able to view everything in a new context that made sense to me. I was able to observe without judgment. I saw how everyone acts out specific, self-chosen roles in a play on their own stage. Basically I became more independent; I did not have to have someone in my life if I did not choose to, nor did I have to pretend to be someone I was not. Although it seemed like new revelations were coming every day, one of the most pronounced happened in a dream almost two months later. In this dream, Christ came to me, took me by the hand, and led me on a journey to God. I have since tried to put this dream into words many times, and although each time it gets a little easier, I can still find no words to really describe what I saw. I will, however, relate the parts that I can. It is difficult to describe a process where there are no words as yet defined (many authors try to create new words to describe their process, but I would like to avoid that, since in my view a new vocabulary confuses things).

On our journey, Christ took me through seven different dimensions to God's resting place in the Seventh Heaven. Each of the Seven Heavens was different and yet the same somehow. It is, I suppose, that the forms kept becoming more and more vague, yet more encompassing. I am not sure exactly what I expected to see, maybe a man on a throne; whatever it was, I didn't see it. To put it simply, since I have no idea how to make it more complex, Christ told me that the Seventh Heaven was God. I nodded in understanding, although I doubt that I really understood.

At this point it was conveyed to me that God, in order to increase His joy, decided to create a "fantasy experience" for Himself. This could be accomplished by creating another dimension (the Sixth Heaven); its creation was accomplished in much the same way as we dream. In this new dimension, God created separate entities in His likeness but with more form. Through these new forms God could play and experience His new world.

These newly formed beings soon decided that they too would like to have more fantasy in their lives and they dreamily created the Fifth Heaven. Like their creator, they separated themselves into their likeness but with more form. This process was continued with progressively more density until the First Heaven was formed. The First Heaven is known as our universe, the world we live in. So we are actually in the First Heaven, where we are given the opportunity to experience maximum separation from the Seventh Heaven or God. With this separation we experience more definition of form than within any other heaven, i.e., we are solid beings living in a solid world.

To clarify and make things much more complex at the same time, we are still God and reside in the Seventh Heaven, but we are also just pretending not to be God and live in the First Heaven.

Christ explained to me that the First Heaven (our universe) was created so we may experience certain "fantasies" not available in any other Heaven, and respectively, each other Heaven has its own "fantasies." Because we are pretending to be the furthest away from God, our games and rules on this planet are without a doubt the most complex of any other recreational dimension. Our universe is considered to be the most challenging of God's recreational realms because of its associated denseness.

Christ then told me some of the basic rules, which help explain more of what this recreational planet is all about. Having the awareness of the rules may help change our perception of why we are here. These rules are not new, just this way of expressing them. Previously these rules have been somewhat hidden and handed down by word of mouth from master to initiate. But, because I cannot keep a secret, I am sharing my insights with the prayer and hope that this knowledge might increase the quality of our lives here on Earth.

Knowing the rules opens the doors we hide behind that prevent us from seeing who we really are. We use many excuses to keep these doors closed; we use fear, ignorance, stasis, hate, and group consensus to keep ourselves confined in our self-made boxes with what we think are permanently locked doors. The first step in this process of self-discovery, of discovering who or what we are pretending to be, is to turn the doorknob to see if it is really locked.

Please remember that like all things on this planet, this book is written by someone who still is bound by the rules of the First Heaven, and the only way to really comprehend this knowledge is by opening the doors and finding the light. I have come to realize that because of God's love for us He wants to reveal all of Himself to us. It is only our own little egos that prevents this relationship. As the rules are understood, you will undoubtedly have a greater insight into the teachings of every master who has ever graced this soil. (As you may have noticed, I just presented my first contradiction with language. God is not a He, nor is God a place.)

Sometimes concepts like these are best understood with a metaphor. So to present this another way, let me tell a story about a little boy.

## The Journey

Once there was a little boy who loved to play. He would rise early in the morning and play all day until bedtime. His parents bought him many toys, including the most current on the market, and therefore he always had something new to experience.

Life was great for this little boy. He had no kids to play with that were his own age, so his toys became his friends. Each of his tin soldiers had names and he would hold very adult conversations with each of them. He loved them all like brothers and could hardly wait until it was time to see them again.

This went on for months until one day he realized he was bored with all these childish games. He had a feeling that he was missing something in life, but he couldn't quite put his finger on what it was. He knew he had everything he could possibly want, yet he was dissatisfied.

One day as he was sitting and talking to one of his soldiers, one of them piped up and asked what all those things were next to his house. The little boy quickly turned his head to see what the soldier was pointing at. He looked and smiled and told them it looked like a forest. All his life he had played so hard that he had never seen the forest next to his house.

He sat staring at the forest for hours and was full of curiosity coupled with fear. What was lurking in the forest? What new adventures awaited him there? He knew he needed to see what was in there, but couldn't decide if he wanted to take his tin soldiers with him for protection or go it alone. Since it was getting close to bedtime, he decided to sleep on it and tomorrow he would venture into this new world.

The next morning came much too early for the little boy. He was still tired, as the sun rose above the horizon, and so he decided this would be a good morning to sleep in. When he arose at noon, he realized it was too late in the day to start a new adventure. Maybe tomorrow.

As the sun rose the following morning, the little boy was awakened by a voice. The voice was calling him to the forest. It was a voice like he never heard before, offering a real sense of assurance. He knew he was ready for this adventure and jumped out of bed. He felt calm, eager, and courageous. He ran to his closet and threw on his red Winnie-the-Pooh hooded shirt and pants, grabbed his sword for protection, and ran out the door.

As he went outside, he found that he was immediately surrounded by his tin soldiers. They had voted and decided they would accompany him because a knight could not go on a crusade without an army. In formation with the little boy leading, they all marched toward the forest.

The forest was unduly dark, as the trees reaching for the sky prevented the light from kissing the ground. The little boy's heart was racing, and he felt like it was resting in his stomach instead of his chest. He looked at his army and saw they too were wide-eyed, but they all continued marching in search of their Holy Grail.

As they walked, the little boy grew more and more uneasy. He had an eerie feeling that he was being watched. He kept spinning around and walking backwards to see if he could catch a glimpse of the thing that was watching them. He did not know quite what to do: should he keep walking forward or run like hell back home. His decision was made for him when he heard a thrashing in the forest.

Within an instant, he and his troops were surrounded by gigantic, fire-breathing dragons. There was no place to run. Immediately his tin soldiers encircled the little boy; they were now in their element. They presented the business ends of their swords to the dragons and began defending their knight. The battle went on for hours and was very fierce. But, alas, when it was finally over, the dragons had won. All of the tin soldiers lay in molten piles on the burnt ground. Tears poured from the boy's eyes as he realized his friends were gone.

The little boy, who had just sat and watched this battle, was now in very serious trouble as the dragons came towards him step by step. The little boy's mind raced as he quickly tried to review his options. No answer manifested and he could now feel the heat of the dragon fire. There was no place to run, and he had lost his sword and saw that it, too, had melted. He realized he was greatly outnumbered. "Yes," he thought, "it's all over." He realized he had gone too far and was in way over his head.

The little boy opened his arms to the dragons, gave up, and prepared for his impeding doom. Just as he did that, he heard that voice again, the one that had woken him up that morning. Except this time it was chanting some sort of incantation. With that, the little boy was encompassed in a beautiful orange light.

He did not know what was happening to him, but it did not matter too much because the dragons were now upon him. In unison, the dragons took a big breath and all snorted their fire at him. The fire engulfed him, but he did not feel heat or discomfort. The orange light had saved him from a fiery grave.

As he stood there in amazement at his great stroke of luck, he noticed that everything was changing. The dragons and the forest were disappearing and he was being transported through the air; he seemed to be heading for a fierce river.

Splash! The little boy found himself propelled through the white waters, heading full tilt down the stream and swallowing mouths full of water. As the trees on the bank whizzed by, he had no idea where he was or where he was going, but he knew innately that he was once again in over his head. He did the only thing he knew how to do—kick and scream.

He was going under for the third time when a hand reached down, grabbed him, and towed him to shore. He could not see who or what was on the other end of the hand.

Once on the shore, he passed out from exhaustion. Later, when he awoke, he found he was bedded down in a primitive hut. As he surveyed the hut, he could make out assorted masks and twisted ropes in designs hanging on the walls; as he became more aware he heard muffled sounds coming from outside.

He didn't know what to do. Should he be brave and stick his head out of the hut or should he stay put where he knew he was safe and warm? And where was his mamma when he needed her most? He decided that his only choice was to be brave, so he gathered up his blankets, went to the corner furthest away from the door, sat down, and covered his head. Remembering his melted friends he thought, "maybe tomorrow." As he sat there huddled up, he noticed that the sounds were getting louder. Just then, with a snap, the blankets were pulled away from him. He saw quickly that he was surrounded by a group of beautiful, naked girls. Naked! He rubbed his eyes and looked again.

When the girls grabbed him and pulled him outside, he was still so stunned that he didn't put up much of a fight. He began to struggle only when the girls stripped the clothes from his body and tied him to a post in the center of the village. Once tied, the girls sat in front of him and kept pointing and giggling as though they had never seen a penis before. The little boy felt humiliated.

He didn't know what to do this time; he was trapped. However, he heard the voice again, and this time with the voice also came a bolt of lightening that struck the rope binding his hands. He was free. He quickly ran and grabbed a spear and became head of this tribe.

It was great. The girls worshipped him for both his magic and his power. Now he was the only dressed person in the village and he would have the girls parade their naked bodies in front of him for hours at a time. He was having a great time; anything he wanted was his. He stayed on as King for quite awhile, until one day he decided this was a rather boring existence. Something was missing. He knew he needed a new quest.

He grabbed his spear, said good-bye to his subjects, and took off to discover where the river would lead him. He fought his way through the thorny bushes bordering the river, following its course. That night as he was resting, he looked at his legs and saw that they were torn to shreds. He knew that tomorrow he would need to find some way to protect himself from this wild natural environment.

When morning came, he went into the adjacent hills and found some soft grayish rock. He took the rock and pounded it into sheets and made some armor for himself. This should protect him on his journey as long as he didn't meet any dragons. So back to the river he marched.

On his trek back to the river, he spied a cave. He had never seen a cave before and his curiosity drew him closer and closer to its gigantic mouth. As he peered inside he saw a beauty that was indescribable. The colors, the giant icicles, and the immenseness of it took him further inside. Touching the wall with one hand and stepping very carefully, he walked on, in awe of everything he saw. It was an experience he hadn't known possible.

He walked until the cave forked. One path was dark and dreary and the other had a pink glow at its end. He wasn't sure which way to go. The dark path looked like it might be more fun and hold many adventures, but the pink one was more beautiful with a certain peace about it. After all the danger he had already been through, he decided on the pink path.

As he walked confidently up the pink path, he heard a voice. The voice sounded somewhat familiar and was calling his name. He increased his gait almost out of instinct in order to find the source of this voice. As he walked (or almost ran), he noticed the light becoming stronger and the voice becoming louder. He was getting excited because he knew he had chosen the right path; this was going to be his best adventure yet.

As he rounded the final corner, he saw the end of the cave; a very bright light sifted into the cave from the new world outside, and he saw a figure of a person calling his name. He took off running as fast as his little legs could carry him. As he approached the person, his face lit up in recognition. He ran and jumped into her arms. It was his mother.

———

The question, "What is real?" must be asked if we are to understand the circle we are in. To the little boy in the story, his perception of reality was changed with each adventure. Was each adventure self-manufactured? Did he pretend to walk in the forest and meet the fire-breathing dragons or was it real for him?

As each person looks hard at his or her life, they must ask the same question. Do we pretend we are poor or wealthy, sick or healthy, unhappy or happy, and separate from God? Do we create fire-breathing dragons to motivate us into new circles—new adventures—or just to add spice into our current life? Do we also find that within each adventure we try to conceptualize our role such as: hero, heroine, man, woman, explorer, etc.?

And finally, as the story shows, he escaped his circles by jumping into the arms of his mother. The mother is symbolic of God.

This story sets a basic premise for the rest of this book, wherein I will try to point out that each never-ending circle has its own unique adventure. Not only are the adventures different, but also there are changes in perceptional reality, changes in the rules of each circle, different rewards, punishments, and changes in what is considered right action.

In the next chapter, I will discuss these aspects and some of the games we play with our minds when housed within a circle. Specifically, how we pretend that our circle is real.

# Chapter 3
## The Game

Now that I have presented the thesis of this book in the preceding chapters, I ask the question: who would want to read and understand this information. I'm presenting this material with the foregone conclusion that the reader is someone just like me. As such, we have undergone many trials in our lives and made decisions that have abruptly altered the course of our lives; we have desperately tried to find a part of ourselves that seemed to be missing. We have read self-help books, looked intensely into many different programs, and followed the teachings of different gurus—all of which offered to give us a magic remedy that would make us feel complete. As yet our thirst has not been quenched. We pick up this book thinking that the answer may lie within its pages, yet knowing intuitively that we will not find it this time either. But that is okay; all we really want anyway is a direction, a clue to find out who we really are. Basically, we are people who are not afraid to delve deeply inside ourselves, to ask unanswerable questions and then seek the answer. We are seekers who are not afraid to look into a mirror at the place just behind our eyes.

As a writer, I am not looking for people to follow my beliefs. I am, however, looking for companions who are walking their own path. So, I cannot give precise instructions, because that would direct everyone to follow my path, but I can give generalizations for the purpose of altering perception. Altering an individual's perceptions will almost always bring a new phase of growth; this is usually the primary purpose of healers, facilitators, therapists, or writers.

As I searched intently for my path, I felt that a part of me was dead, and that I had housed within my body a gigantic void that weighed me down and impeded my life. However, when I received a glimpse of my path I was alive, really alive: I was full, complete, and everything in the universe was perfect. These times are very special and help motivate me through the dead periods. Although I love the alive periods, I am reminded that it is really the dead periods that motivate me toward growth. This is true as a generalization; if we are broke, we become motivated to go to work, if we feel stupid, we are motivated to learn, and so on. Of course, this is all dependent on the desire to change.

What are the events that give us clues to our path? What gives us that fleeting feeling of aliveness? I have found myself walking by a mirror, glancing in it, and seeing a stranger. Then in a moment I recognize myself and feel a momentary elation of discovering who I really am. All my preconceived notions of what I look like disappear when I think I am looking at someone else. The same thing happens when we look at ourselves without any preconceived notions and see God; we experience momentary elation. Other events that might give us this same sense of elation could be when we look at a tree, watch a sunset, or sit overlooking an ocean. During these events, our perception shifts for a moment and we become God-like—we uncover a God-trait within ourselves and relish in that momentary recognition of who we really are—we recognize that person beyond our normal thoughts, feelings, and emotions. The purpose of our spiritual path is to strip away those erroneous concepts that keep us from seeing the God within.

It seems logical that if we can have fleeting moments of seeing or being the God within us, then the possibility exists for that to be continuous. It should be possible to expand those times from nanoseconds to minutes to years to a lifetime.

Most of us see those experiences of touching the God within as a novelty, unaware that the opposite, separation from God, should be the novelty. However, very few people are enamored enough with the associated feeling of touching God to dedicate their lives to the pursuit of increasing those moments.

Again, I am making the assumption that the reader has had similar experiences and knows the feeling of non-separation from God. For anyone who has experienced that feeling, they are faced with a similar dilemma as I: how is that feeling conveyed to others? Even though many poets have attempted to voice this wordless sensation, it remains a feeling beyond words.

Only by intuition can we prove the thesis of this book: we are God at play in another dimension while pretending to be separate. Yet, for those of us who have felt our oneness with God (at least in brief episodes), the belief does exist that it is our natural state, and likewise, there is some force, some state of being preventing us from realizing God on a continuous basis. It is those separators that we must look at and alleviate if we wish to become God-realized.

These separators are what I refer to as our never-ending circles, which are reinforced by specific games housed snugly within. The games we play are based on the player's perceptions of their role within the particular circle. So, if I perceive myself as a man, then that role helps lock me into certain "manly" games, which in turn locks me into specific circles. My "man-ness" provides the basic rules of how I am expected to play certain games. (I have chosen to use the words play and game to represent our involvement, because if this is a recreational planet as suggested, then that is normally how we choose to recreate—I am not using these terms to make light of some of our plights.)

When we are fortunate enough to experience a change in perception, our games and circles also change. The change in perception alters the way we obey the rules. That does not necessarily mean that a change in perception will allow us to leave a game or circle, although it might; generally, however, it just lets us play at a different level.

As an oversimplified example, let's look at video games. If someone develops a new video game, then the people who choose to play that game initially will read the basic rules of the game, combine it with their personal experience with similar types of games, and will usually perform rather crudely in their initial tries. However, as they continue to play their perception will shift, allowing them to better understand the nuances of the game (which is classically called a "learning curve"). As their perception shifts, their scores will be higher.

Therefore, as we enter into a new game or circle, the first things we must learn are the rules. There are basically two ways rules are learned, either by instruction or experience. As a general rule, we learn the fundamental rules by instruction. The rules for the games of life are handed down via our family, culture, church, friends, or societal laws. Then, through experience, we modify those laws relative to how we perceive "self."

The person who understands all the nuances of a particular game becomes a master of that game. As a master, he or she can play with variations of the rules, while the novice is forced to play with the very limiting, fundamental rules. Both the master and the novice are playing the same game, yet somehow, the rewards are different. The master gets to play with self-concepts of power, control, and manipulation, while the beginner plays with self-concepts such as failure, frustration, being manipulated, and the discovery of the subtle rules. If forced to play directly against each other, the master can feel absolute power and the beginner can experience futility until he or she gives up or moves into a position of mastery. But if either are allowed to play with an equal, they will both experience much more enjoyment. A bond can be formed between players because their perception of reality is based on the same rules.

The first step in any game is to learn the basic rules. The next step is to learn more advanced rules and accepted strategies, and then to develop personal strategies. As we learn and experience the rules, the game takes on more life. So within any game, whether it is checkers or the game of life, we find a continuum of players. On the one end we find the novice, on the other, the master. The primary difference between the two ends of the continuum is knowledge of the game. This can be expanded further to say that at one end we have those who do not play, and on the other end, one who plays perfectly, the master. The perfect master is the one whose actions are one with the game; he or she experiences no surprises, for they know every move and counter-move before it happens. As can be well-imagined, there are not too many "opponents" to play once this stage is reached. Of course, being God, we are all at this stage, so to increase our play, to allow us to play with others, we pretend not to be perfect masters.

The essence of this game of life is that we pretend not to be a master and then establish mastery as our goal. Isn't the paradox just beautiful? It is an impossibility to remain a beginner in any game, therefore a modification and advanced understanding of the rules—which is a movement toward mastery—happens as an evolutionary process. Whether the change in perception is radical enough to cause a move to perfect mastery is another question; it is a question of relativity, since any modification of experience will allow one to look like a master when viewed by a beginner. In other words, anyone who stumbles through their first attempt of a game will have more experience than someone who has not and will, therefore, appear like a master of that game to the beginner.

To many of us it is a strange paradox, for we can look around at many of the people we know and see that it is apparently untrue—these people do not appear to be striving towards mastery. Welcome to the world of judgment. It is relatively easy to judge someone else's actions, to look at them and think that these people are not moving toward any sort of mastery and may even be going backward. The majority of people on this planet are very good at pretending they are not masters, and they will create situations to prove their belief a fact. But, as an observer, we really have no way of knowing what circle or game another is trying to master. Granted, there are many people who do not know the rules of our particular circle or game and some who will be less adept than we are, but the paradox exists: everyone—in their own way and in their own game and circle—is moving toward mastery. It is only our judgment, our egotistic desire to be better than others (which is part of how we were taught to play), that lets us see anyone as a non-master.

As an example, look at the homeless person. Our judgment might tell us that this person is a lost soul and because he or she doesn't have a house, a car, or food is neither a master nor are they moving toward mastery. But most are very good at what they do. They have learned the rules of their current life situation; they have modified and adapted them, and have moved toward mastery. I know that if I was forced to walk in their shoes, I couldn't do it; but, then again, it is not my "game." They would have trouble walking in my shoes also.

We all have the desire to move to the level of mastery. This desire is comparable to a genetic drive much like our sex drive, except the move to mastery never seems to be gratified. With the sex drive, one orgasm and it diminishes (unless sexual experiences are a never-ending circle). With the mastery drive, at every new growth level, we see new areas to grow into. Mastery is therefore somewhat elusive, but the drive towards it leads us to believe that once we have attained it, we will experience unlimited power, wealth, and happiness. The real advantage to mastery is acquiring the ability to explore and expose one's limits, which speeds up the process back to God. Two ways to speed this process are by entering wholeheartedly into another's experiences and letting the other person push us to our limits (Carlos Castenadas defines this process as petty tyrantism) or we can create new experiences for ourselves. Most non-masters can only deal with one or two people or situations at a time, while masters—because they love complexity—strive to learn from as many people and situations as possible, all at the same time.

A good example of the petty tyrant scenario is the one where we play the role of being the victim. We do this by convincing others that they have more knowledge, control, or power than we do. Total power in this context is defined as the ability to have another person do exactly what we want done, when we want it done. If they accept the premise, then a unique environment can be created, one where another person or group of people pretend to have complete control over our destiny. We find petty tyrants— the person or entity to whom we give our power—in our schools, governments, cults, churches, or even work. On a personal level, we experience these tyrants as abusers, rapists, and terrorists. This scenario requires that two or more people join together who are working on opposite perceptual concepts. The petty tyrant needs to find someone who is trying to conceptualize inner strength, passiveness, or a lack of discipline, while the victim needs to find the person who is conceptualizing outer power, aggressiveness, or self-control. If the petty tyrant pushes too hard, then the victim may give up and collapse into the pain.

The helpless game is the foundation of most religions. Many religions want us to believe that their minister, priest, or rabbi is our go-between to God. As such, we pretend that we are helpless in our attempts to communicate with God while also pretending that someone else has a more direct contact. These "men or women of God" can be found trying to conceptualize outer power, aggressiveness, or self-control; while most of them will teach inner strength, passiveness, or discipline.

Within most religious structures, the attainment of enlightenment (or heaven) is our goal. Unfortunately, most religions promise the reward will come after we die. According to our paradox, the game still requires us to pretend we don't have heaven already.

Churches, therefore, are a very valuable playground and tend to draw players to them that wish to participate in the church's particular form of structured games. However, most people striving for mastery become easily bored because they find the church games too simple and repetitious. The ideal church for master initiates would allow the exploration of many different experiences; it would allow its members to explore their limits more fully. Support from the group would remind us that we are just recreating, hopefully remove some of the heaviness and intensity of life. The problem we generally encounter is that we get so wrapped up in some of our actions that we forget to enjoy them.

Although it is seemingly difficult to accept ourselves as God, it is usually more difficult to accept anyone else as God. Almost all of the common games require that first we pretend we are not God and second that we pretend that no one else is either. The concept that we're not all God allows us to pretend that power is never divided equally giving rise to dynamic relationships where the power shifts.

The idea of relationships brings up one of the most difficult assumptions made in this book. (I will develop this further throughout the later chapters, but my primary assumption is that God always acts from a position of love.) If this assumption is true, then we (as Gods pretending not to be Gods) also do everything from the basis of love. This is a hard concept to understand since we can look around our world and see hate-mongers. So let's define love as a non-judgmental, nonconditional response in which one person supports another either by appropriate action or appropriate non-action.

As an example, in a marriage relationship where love exists, both parties intuitively know that the other person is going to support them in their endeavors. Does the same thing happen in abusive relationships? Our immediate response is probably to say that an abusive relationship is not a loving relationship, but if my love assumption is correct, then we must admit that even in an abusive relationship both parties are acting from a position of love. No matter how skewed we think the motivations may be, both are supporting the roles and perceptions of the other person. For example, the abused person is learning about inner strength and passiveness, while the abuser is learning about loss of control and aggressiveness. As sad as we may think these actions are, it is probably the only way these people can learn these lessons or have these experiences. Usually, both parties pray that they could leave their particular never-ending circle. It is not to say that a person should stay in this type of relationship for the lesson, but history tells us that they will until their perception changes enough to realize that they don't have to stay in that particular circle. On the other hand, we see many abused people who go from one abuser to another, never understanding that their perception of themselves as victim comprises half of the relationship.

The definition of love as "warm snugglies," as handed down by convention (or Madison Avenue), has to be perceived differently. Under our new definition, such things as abuse, murder, and persecution can be seen as acts of love. This point is currently being debated relative to euthanasia (mercy killings) of terminally ill people. Using the old definitions of love, killing someone is not love; but under my definition it could be if performed for the person's higher good. Am I advocating the use of violence as an expression of love? DEFINITELY NOT. This example is to show how a change in perception can change definitions and move us to a place of non-judgment.

How we perceive self-love and love of others is a key to how we perceive our circles and games. I will discuss in later chapters how we use these concepts to define all of our relationships. I also will discuss how to use the dynamics of a relationship to determine which circle we are in and then how to use those dynamics to free ourselves once and for all from the never-ending circles that bind us.

To reiterate, the first step is to know we are all God and all of our games and circles are played out under the premise that we are separate from God.

Metaphorically, this can be expressed by a little story called:

## The Descent

The clouds opened wide as the eagle descended into the atmosphere of earth. It was his first visit to this planet and he was excited about his new adventure. As he saw the rocky terrain below, he stretched out his mighty wings and soared under the adjacent clouds miles above the earth. He was traveling so fast now that the feathers of his wings were vibrating in ecstasy.

The air was cooler under the clouds than above, so he was glad he had packed his winter underwear. He had heard many stories of this place, but he was not quite sure what to bring with him.

According to the stories, he knew this would be his best adventure to date. He had been planning for this trip for quite awhile and had to pass many tests to assure his birdhood before he was even allowed to consider a trip to this planet. He knew he was very lucky to be here.

This was a beautiful place, and he could see why so many of his teachers loved it. He now understood why it was so difficult to get here, the teachers wanted to have a place they could go that was not over-populated. It was their own little recreational planet. Although he had not explored the whole of the planet, he already liked the beauty and the coolness, which was really refreshing after the last place he had been, which was hot and plain.

Off in the distance, he spotted some majestic mountains, so he dipped his right wing and side slipped until he was pointing straight in their direction. He put his head down, and like a rocket, he headed towards these colorful peaks; it looked like a perfect place for an eagle to hang out.

In no time at all, he was upon them, weaving in and around the peaks, when he spied a peculiar cloud formation that was dark and lacy-looking. He flew towards it with his head cocked in curiosity. As he approached it, he found himself speeding up; he was being sucked into a black hole. He immediately put his wings in reverse and tried to back up with all his force, but the power of the hole was too great and he ended up pummeling beak over talon into the darkness.

The power he encountered as he met the darkness knocked him out, causing him to experience a state of amnesia. Once inside the abyss, he was sucked down and transformed; the power stripped him of his eagle rights of passage.

He awoke from this experience with tears in his eyes, a cry on his lips, and hunger. Out of instinct, he searched for and found a breast and started suckling milk. When he came to his senses, after a few weeks, he realized he was with his family and that his mother was a beautiful mouse, who took good care of her family.

During his early life in the nest he learned many lessons about all the things he needed to be afraid of. This was a rather easy lesson to learn, since half of his brothers and sisters had already become someone's dinner. But he learned well his lessons of survival and became an adult.

Within the mouse community, he was known for his cunning and was asked to become the teacher for the younger mice. He eagerly accepted, because this meant he was allowed into the community libraries which were reserved for the mouse elders and scholars.

His favorite section in the library was the one that housed all the great writings from the noted philosophers of the past. He had heard many of the stories they had written, but it was different to read their works without another's interpretation. He especially loved the ones who wrote about meta-mousics, and he grew to believe that there was a life beyond mousehood.

He would check out one of these books and sit and read under his favorite tree for hours at a time. Often his mind would take off into fantasy and he would imagine he was an eagle soaring high above the earth. Eventually he would return to his senses and realize he was just a mouse, and he would go back to his mundane duties.

# Chapter 4
## Building the Model

It wasn't too many years ago that spiritual seekers hid in caves striving to discover their essence, while at the same time, scientists were busy hiding in their laboratories trying to reduce life to a simple enough form in the hope of understanding nature. Both groups thought that if they could understand one part of nature then all their questions regarding the whole would be answered, but it did not manifest that way. Many ascetics died in their caves without understanding themselves, and science kept splitting the atom only to find that it could be reduced even further.

In the mid-1800s, a group came together in an attempt to impact society by presenting a case for thought that would turn away from reductionism—breaking into parts in order to discover the whole—to vitalism (holism)—a holistic approach which believes that the whole is greater than the sum of the parts. This group, who called themselves "Transcendentalists," included such now famous philosophers and writers as Emerson, Thoreau, Whitman, and Alcott. An example of this reform was written by Emerson who said,

> Man is a stream whose source is hidden. Always our being is descending into us from we know not whence... I am constrained every moment to acknowledge a higher origin for events than the will I call mine (Emerson, <u>Emerson's Essays. 1926</u>, p.189).

Almost all of these transcendentalists have literary works whose messages are alive today. These works are considered to contain the classics of wisdom and they are the basis for much of today's "New Thought." Although they were trying to remold the philosophy of the world, it seemed to have very little effect on the medical community who were still bleeding their patients with leeches in order to cure them of their ills (this is still being done) or the science community who were actively pursuing Descartism: proving their thesis by rigor and in strictly linear fashion.

One health care dissident who had the courage to break away from conventional thought was D. D. Palmer when he established chiropractic in the late 1800s as an avenue for the vitalistic approach to health care . Dr. Palmer writes:

> *That which I named "Innate" (born with) is a segment of that intelligence which fills the universe. This universal, all-wise, is metamerized, divided into metameres as needed by each individualized being. This somatome of the whole, never sleeps nor tires, recognizes neither darkness nor distance, and is not subject to material laws or conditions. It continues to care for and direct the functions of the body as long as the soul holds the body and spirit together.*
>
> *Innate's existence and consciousness are not dependent upon its body, no more than we are on the house we live in. It is invincible, cannot be injured or destroyed by material changes. It is invulnerable, is not subject to traumatic or toxic injuries, is not subordinate to material substance. (Palmer, The Science, Art, and Philosophy of Chiropractic. 1910, p 491)*

One hundred years later, this approach to health care is active and is just within the last twenty years being proved by the old methods of rigor and linearality.

Science also had its dissidents. At the turn of the century, scientists such as Max Planck, Albert Einstein, Neils Bohr, Louis de Brogie, and Edwin Schroeder gave us Quantum Physics and the Theory of Relativity. Then Benoit Mandelbrot gave us Chaos Theory, David Bohm gave us the Unmanifest Plane, Nobelist Roger Sperry developed the Concept of Casual Potency, and today many more are helping us apply new holistic concepts to our lives. These "Quantum thinkers" all have one thing in common: they are magnificent writers. These great thinkers of our time participate in virtually every discipline, including religion, physics, chemistry, medicine, chiropractic, and psychology, reiterating in their own special ways that everything is connected and follows a pre-established order.

More specifically, Quantum Theory points out that the experimenter and the experimentee are intertwined and therefore each has an affect on the other. The Theory of Relativity points out that what we deem as real is based on a specific point of reference. Chaos Theory claims that there is always an implicate order and things only appear chaotic because the true order is unknown. The Unmanifest Plane is similar to the Zen Buddhist's uncarved block, i.e., that a vacuum has the potential to be anything. And in the Concept of Casual Potency, Sperry says that thought-forms within the mind contain a certain amount of power and do cause things to happen in proportion to the amount of power they contain.

It is not my intent to discuss these theories at length, because there are currently many books written on their impact, rather I will use these theories to explain a model for finding spiritual freedom.

For example, we can use the concepts of Quantum Physics to define two metaphysical terms: enlightenment and endarkenment. By religious standards we define these terms synonymously with heaven and hell, good and evil, and so on. In our model, we will see how those terms are a constant part of our growth process. To use Quantum Physics to help define these terms we need to create a simile. In physics, an atom has rings of electrons circling it, and it is more than the total of the parts that make up the sum, which enables us to define that particular molecule. None of the rings are more important than any other. As an electron moves to an outer ring, light is received, and as it falls to an inner ring, light is given off. The process of an electron moving to an outer ring could be classified as enlightenment since it must take light (energy) in before it can make its quantum leap to the next ring. Likewise, the move to a lower ring could be classified as an endarkenment process.

We can now expand our electron model and pretend that our consciousness is this electron. And like the electron, which is always going through a process of change from enlightenment to endarkenment and back again, each thought that we have either adds or subtracts from the energy of the whole system. From physics, we know that movement to the outer rings is an infinite process because there is apparently always one more ring, while movement to an inner ring seems to be limited and leads to a very unstable ion.

Using this concept as one of the basis for our model, if we can reach the outer rings of our atom, then surely we can be free, or can we? Won't we always be in some type of ring? Maybe, but like all good theories it will depend on how we build our model and define our concepts.

To return to our argument: is there a purpose for our consciousness to go through this enlightenment-endarkenment process? This is a good question, because for centuries philosophers have wondered about the meaning of life. Why are we here? And what are we supposed to do now that we are here? These are very difficult questions, because no matter what we conjure up as possible answers, we can always find exceptions. Since there are exceptions, maybe it is because our initial premise is wrong. An interesting premise that would allow for all our theories and exceptions is that maybe we are not here; maybe we just think we are here. This may be a very valid premise, but is rather hard to substantiate and doesn't help us much as we try to gather enough money to pay next month's rent. However, we could very easily be playing "let's pretend we live on the planet earth."

I prefer the concept that we are here as a form of recreation and as such can experience new things never before experienced. This requires that we create illusions, live within these self-created illusions, and pretend they are real. For the most part, all of us do this very well.

Illusions are nothing more than a redefinition of something that we perceive as being true. So we are able to look at a grouping of electrons and redefine them as a wall or we can look in the mirror and redefine what we see as a real body, and so on. According to the Theory of Relativity, on a broad scope, our redefinitions are based on our vantage point and how we choose to perceive what we are viewing. For instance, if our walls imprison us, then that would be perceived differently than a wall that is just an obstacle.

This reminds me of a little story about a guy who encounters a wall:

## Charlie Meets the Wall

Charlie was becoming very upset and tired with how his life was shaping up. He felt he was in a rut and couldn't climb out of it. No matter what he did, he found that his activities were, to say the least, boring.

Even the weather seemed to mimic his mood. It was a season of very cloudy days where everything looks gray and feels heavier than it actually is.

Charlie wanted things to change; he was tired of the way they were. Yet, he knew that in the final analysis it was up to him to make the change. He was the only one who could change his situation.

He also knew that to make a change required some sort of risk. The bigger the change, the bigger the risk. What could he do other than just go for it.

He had heard that there existed a city not too far away where all the inhabitants were happy, free, and devoutly spiritual. He checked with all his friends, the ministers in his town, and even the library, but he could not find the exact location of this place. The only information he could find was that this city was east of where he already was. Even though he knew he might never find it, or might not even survive the trip, he decided it was worth the risk to seek out this magical place.

So off he went in search of this city. He had barely gotten out of town, however, when he encountered a tremendous wall. The wall must have been twenty feet high, and there was no telling how thick it was. It seemed to go on forever in either direction. Charlie thought it was strange that no one in the town had ever mentioned this wall being there, but he realized that probably no one else in the town had ever ventured this far away. Or if they did, they just found a doorway through the wall and went on their merry way. He needed to do that too.

Upon closer examination of the wall, he discovered it was comprised of gigantic rocks. Was Charlie's dream going to be shattered by an obstacle like this? Was he going to have to return to his old way of life? Charlie stood there in disbelief.

The more he thought about the wall standing in the way of his goals, the angrier he became, until he became so enraged, he ran right at the wall trying to ram his way through it. When Charlie hit the wall, he bounced back about ten feet, which made him angrier. Somewhat dazed and more angry, he tried again, and again he bounced back battered and bruised.

It was at this point that he calmed down and decided to reevaluate his position. He knew he couldn't force his way through this obstacle, but he also knew that his goal was a mandatory objective, so he should find an alternate route.

He quickly realized that since he couldn't force his way through the wall, maybe he could manipulate it. One way to manipulate this obstacle was to simply climb over it. So he started climbing. He was doing pretty well, all things considered, and he was up about seven feet when he slipped and fell off. Each time he tried, he moved up the wall a little further. But the furthest he could manage was about ten feet, just halfway.

Charlie was getting very tired by now, so he looked around to see what his next course of action might be. If he couldn't go over it, then maybe he could go under it. Charlie got on his hands and knees and started digging, but the ground was too hard to even make a dent.

By now, Charlie was becoming desperate. In fact, the more tired he became, the more desperate he was to find a way to get past the wall. He was now so upset he had even forgotten about the city.

He realized that he did have a little rationality left when he decided the easiest solution to his problem would be to just walk around the wall. It might take a little longer, but maybe he wasn't in that big of a hurry after all.

So Charlie started walking, following the perimeter of the wall. He walked and walked, constantly looking for the end or perhaps a hidden door, but the wall just kept on going and going. Charlie was getting tired again, so he sat down. He was sitting looking at the ground when he noticed footprints in the dirt. He became excited; someone had come this way before. He looked again at the footprints and then realized they were his. He had walked in a circle. The wall apparently surrounded the town.

What was he going to do now? He had tried everything: going through the wall, over the wall, under the wall, and now around the wall. He had tried every imaginable way to overcome this great obstacle, but it seemed he was blocked from reaching his dream, regardless of which course of action he chose.

It was at this point that Charlie decided he should take a few minutes and devise a better plan. He started his contemplation by going over in his mind what he had already tried. When he observed himself in action, he started to laugh at himself. He thought he was looking at the funniest comedian in the world. It was real slapstick comedy in its true art form. His desperation to reach his goal had led him to experience a most bizarre set of activities. He had made a complete fool out of himself.

Charlie found that because he was able to laugh at himself, he was able to lighten up considerably.

As he sat there in awe of this great obstacle, he realized he needed outside help. Should he send for a psychologist? Was the wall just a block in his head or a vivid dream? Should he ask a radiologist to x-ray the wall to see how thick and serious this obstruction was? Maybe a scientist could analyze the components of the wall to see if a chemical could burn a hole through it? Would any of these solutions work? Finally he decided he knew the answer was to pray to God for help.

He thought to himself, "How do I want God to help me?" After much thought, he got down on his knees and prayed for rain to wash the wall away. Then as he was taught in church, he sat patiently, waiting for God to answer his prayers.

Sure enough, after a couple of hours, it started to rain. It rained very hard for an hour, but the rain had absolutely no effect on the wall at all, except to maybe clean it. All it really did was to make Charlie wet and cold.

Charlie quickly realized his mistake. He had made an error in judgment. He now knew, though, that he was close to an answer. So he prayed again, but this time he prayed for enough wind to blow the wall down. Then, he waited patiently. All of a sudden, a great gust of wind came up, and blew so hard that it plastered Charlie right up against a tree. However, when the wind stopped and Charlie looked at the wall, nothing had changed.

So what was Charlie to do now? God had answered his prayers, but Charlie figured it was either just too much for God to handle or perhaps he had asked the wrong questions.

Charlie decided he needed to dig deeper to find a solution to his problem, so he went into deep meditation to further contemplate his dilemma. He remembered something he had read—masters have three main qualities: they can laugh at themselves, they are endlessly patient, and they can improvise. He realized that to some degree he had used all three in fighting his obstacle.

Charlie then decided to think back to the start of his day and look closer at his overall objective. When he started recounting all of the events of the day and his thoughts and feelings about them, he started to laugh. The more he thought about it, the more he laughed. He laughed at himself first, then he laughed at his goal, then he roared at the wall. He thought this was the funniest scenario he had ever witnessed.

When Charlie finally stopped laughing, he opened his eyes and the wall was gone as he knew it would be. He broke into laughter again and went home knowing he had achieved a new level of understanding. Because he gave up trying to conquer the wall, and he was able to laugh about it, his goal was realized.

As previously stated, our consciousness pretends to be an electron, and it jumps from ring to ring in an enlightenment-endarkenment process. We now can define what the rings represent. We have stated that the whole concept of atoms, rings, and electrons exists only because we are pretending to be separate from God. Let's define the rings themselves as our "minor pretend games." Because there are infinite rings, there could be an infinite number of minor pretend games. Since infinity is rather hard to work with in creating a model, we will need to group these games into categories.

So far, we have two main categories of games which we call "major" and "minor." The major one is that we pretend we are not God. In the minor ones, we pretend we are stupid or smart, rich or broke, lonely or loved, and dualities on infinitum. All of these minor games allow us to perceive different types of experiences. If I look into my bank account and see millions of dollars, my perception of this experience will be inherently different than if I see nothing in my account. The fascinating concept is that the experiences are interrelated and allow us to play the same minor pretend game but from different perspectives. Let me explain, I can not pretend I am rich if no one is poor, I can not pretend I am smart if no one else is stupid, nor can I pretend to be lonely if everyone loves me.

One of the oldest models is found in the Hindu religion, which groups these minor pretend games into categories. This model is known as the Chakra system. The Chakra model was developed by the Hindus thousands of years ago with a Chakra being an energy point in the energy body that vibrates at a unique frequency. There are seven primary Chakras housed within a person's energy body, each representing a specific life process. The goal of the initiate, through meditation and proper action, is to become aware of all the lessons of each chakra starting with the root chakra and continuing until they reach the seventh chakra at the top of head where "enlightenment" is realized.

Following is a list of the seven primary Chakras and related associations of our minor pretend games as I originally learned them:

ROOT CHAKRA (groin area) survival needs
ABDOMINAL CHAKRA (lower abdomen) sexuality, relationships
SOLAR PLEXUS (upper abdomen) personal power
HEART CHAKRA (heart area) love, compassion
THROAT CHAKRA (throat area) internal dialogue, psychicism
THIRD EYE CHAKRA (between eyes) ideal perception
CROWN CHAKRA (top of head) Oneness–enlightenment

At the base of the spine in the first Chakra lies a pool of consciousness which the Hindus call Kundalini (the snake). The way to attain enlightenment, according to the Kundalini Model, is by releasing this energy thereby allowing it to slither up the spine. Colton, in his book Kundalini West, claims that it is an energy that is fiery and serpent-like and is housed in a bundle of nerves on the tiny bridge between the rectum and the sexual organs.

Although the Chakra Model offers a very good theory to use as a base for the model we are going to create, it does have some inherent problems. This model teaches that we need to work through the lessons of each Chakra in ascending order so we can eventually reach spiritual enlightenment. This could be a great never-ending game, because we can conceivably fabricate as many particular lessons as we wish and the process could be endless (infinite rings). Part of the concept of Kundalini requires that we consider that life offers us problems to solve, instead of mysteries to be experienced or recreation to be enjoyed.

However, if we are already enlightened and are just pretending not to be, the concept of trying to learn specific lessons and therefore reach a point of enlightenment is unnecessary. If, in fact, we are really not here to learn lessons and this planet isn't really a school, then this is not a very satisfying model.

Once a person studies and participates in the classical Chakra theory as previously eluded to, three things become apparent. First, because of the tendency to view spiritual attainment through the ego. Many people think they are already at the Crown Chakra. Second, if we look hard at the lessons we are learning, we can associate them with more than one Chakra, which is a contradiction if our progression up the spine is linear. Third, the corresponding Chakra on the opposite side of the heart offers similar lessons to be learned, but from a different focus. There are some redeeming values to the Chakra model, however, which I will incorporate into the new model.

In my dream, which was discussed in Chapter Two, God created the Seven Heavens by adding one more dimension each time. Therefore our model should be made up of seven main components (like the seven Chakras), and at the least, each component should be a replica of the Heaven it represents. Each of these Heavens represent a "quanta" or packet of energy. These packets of energy are the fuel that runs the never-ending circles of that particular Heaven. To try to clarify the language, metaphorically, each of these Heavens can be represented by an electron ring in our Quantum model and each ring represents a grouping of minor pretend games. So, basically, the individual Heavens, the electron rings, and the minor pretend games are all the same thing for the sake of this discussion.

Whereas in classical Chakra theory we move through the lessons of each chakra in linear fashion, we know that we can incorporate Mandelbrot's Chaos Theory by focusing on a specific ring within a non-linear format where each ring identifies a grouping of minor pretend games (see fig. 1, pg. 36).

In a classical linear approach, we create a starting point and move systematically along a predestined course. In Chaos Theory, the starting point and ending point may or may not be on the course and the course itself may appear random. In our model, the beginning and ending point are the same—Godhood. Obviously trying to move to a point which is the same as the beginning by a linear means is rather difficult, if not impossible. So the object of this model, or if you will, the meaning of life, is to add energy to the electrons (consciousness) in the rings in whatever order our life dictates. If enough energy is added to a specific electron, we could force it into the next ring, and because light is received, we will experience enlightenment. It doesn't matter which ring is focused on, because in reality there is no proper order, it is the enlightenment and endarkenment processes that are important. The purpose of our model is to find freedom by realizing we are one with God.

When we pretend to be separate from God, we also pretend that these rings exist. Conceptually, they are created by withdrawing light from those electrons (our consciousness) and forcing them to take up residence in newly-created rings. The only way to create an endarkenment situation is by reducing the amount of light we receive, thereby creating our reality. This is explained in classical Chakra Theory when each chakra is represented by a different, specific color. When we send white light through a prism, we separate that light into a rainbow of colors, thereby, reducing the light into parts—it no longer looks like white light. These parts give variations to what is perceived as white light. Colored light will alter one's perception of the truth. For example, if we were to stand in a room lit only by red light, the room would look different to our eyes than if we stood in a room illuminated only by green light.

To create another analogy, look at the sun/moon relationship. The moon is dark and does not generate its own light (I hope that is not a new concept for some of us). However, the moon does go through phases from fully enlightened (full moon) to totally dark (new moon). Through all of its phases, the moon does not change. Even in its full phase, when it looks like it is generating its own light, it is only pretending to be enlightened, because it is only reflecting the sun's light.

The Christian religion tries to emphasize the moon's role when it preaches the importance of our being a reflection of Jesus, the Son. To have a model such as Jesus (at least metaphorically) is a wonderful thing, not to use as a reflection, but as way of becoming the Sun. This is also true for Buddha, Krishna, Confucius, Zoroaster, and St. Francis, etc.

To take our analogy a step further, we are actually a sun in that we generate our own light; we are just pretending to be the moon. We, like the moon, can pretend to be the sun all we want, but until we understand we are only pretending to be endarkened and enlightened, we will never return to our natural state of light. To pretend we are something we are not might be fun for awhile, but it is not beneficial in our quest for mastery in the long run.

Before we manifest ourselves on earth, we choose which primary ring we are going to participate in at any particular point in our life. Part of the experience seems to require, for some, that we pretend to hide our primary ring from ourselves which is why this process may be named the "quest." So often people go through their lives thinking they were working on their proper ring, but in fact, they were working on someone else's. Or else they flash back to a different lifetime to a ring they mastered, or somewhat mastered, and they want to relive those experiences. As we look around at all the Gods in our universe, we see many who are seemingly enjoying their ring, and if ours isn't going so well, we have a tendency to try to switch to theirs. As much as we would like to change our particular ring to match someone else's, there will always be another who wishes he or she was in our shoes. The key then is to love and enjoy our particular ring. Obviously the first step in our process is to find out which ring we are in. So, let's define these rings more in depth.

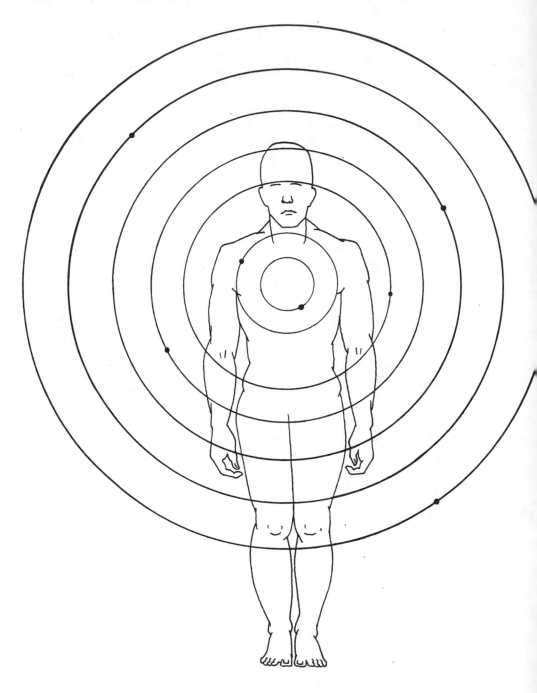

**Fig. 1 Rings of Man**

# Chapter 5

## Survival Ring (First Heaven)

When I use the term "survival" there is a tendency in most people's minds to relate it to eating, having a place to stay, or just simply staying alive. But for the sake of our model, I want to expand the term to include any action which pertains to the physical body.

To enhance the Chakra model, let's place this ring within the Heart Chakra. The reason for this is because our physical heart is the primary determinate that establishes whether we are alive or dead. I think we would all agree that being dead or being alive would represent the ultimate in a ring pertaining to the physical body, and therefore related to survival—life and death struggles. In the broad scope, we created an endarkenment situation for the body to even exist, because that action allowed us to separate ourselves from God. Within each ring (heaven or grouping of minor pretend games) there is also a range of energy, so participants can pretend that the whole model is housed within that particular ring. Therefore, each participant can experience some form of enlightenment and endarkenment within an individual ring. Relative to the ring of survival, we can experience different aspects of endarkenment that lead to deterioration of the body, illness, injury, or at the extreme, death. Enlightenment on the other hand, leads to a sense of well-being and at its ultimate, immortality. Active participants in this ring perform rituals like running, weight-training, and eating properly with the objective of living longer.

Therefore, within this ring we find that our state of health is a primary concern. What is a state of health? For most people indoctrinated into the allopathic medical model it is a state of being without disease. For this reason, medical doctors profess that by killing the uninvited organisms that enter the body, a state of health can be derived. There are two main flaws with this logic: one is that the medicines themselves are uninvited guests, and the other is that many bacteria known to medicine live within the body normally. It is important to realize that within the field of toxicology a medicine's ability to survive is defined by looking at its half-life. A half-life is the period of time when half of the substance is still active. This is the same calculation that science uses to measure radioactivity. The mathematical progression for half-lives is 1, 1/2, 1/4, 1/8, 1/16, 1/32, 1/64, and so forth into infinity. This means that once a drug is introduced into a body, a part of the toxin will always be there. The medical argument is that it will eventually reach a point of ineffectiveness, but what they are saying is that it will get too weak to kill the intended uninvited organism. Yet, the question remains unanswered as to what other changes can be caused by even small amounts of a drug. These other changes are referred to as "side effects."

The interesting thing about pharmaceuticals (and n particular, antibiotics and chemotherapy drugs) is that for the most part they create an endarkenment situation, because they shut off the life force for part of the body with the hope that it's only the part and not the whole will die.

Like most things in this universe, there seems to be a time and a place for everything. One of the messages of this book is that anything taken to excess is going to take us down the road of endarkenment and only by making decisions aimed at creating an enlightenment process will we move to a level of mastery. Many people have shrines in their homes to some God, but in my opinion it should not be a medicine cabinet that, when opened, overflows with empty pill bottles all dedicated to the "Great Medical God of Health." Medicine should be used as the last resort when all vitalistic approaches have failed. I once heard a statistic that 80% of all medical cases will resolve by themselves without any outside intervention. The 20% of problems that require medical attention are primarily serious injuries, not sicknesses. Therefore, 80% of the time that we visit our medical doctor, he or she will either give us a drug or operate and remove some part of us, when if left alone, our body would have healed itself, given enough time. These are truly awesome statistics.

Terrence Bennett, in his book <u>Dynamics of Correction of Abnormal Function</u>, referred to this when he said,

> *This campaign of fear, of hysteria, that is going on in this country is criminal. Hundreds of thousands of breasts have been removed from women. Men and women are driven into doctors' offices for check-ups they do not need. The least little thing happens, it could be cancer. Everything they can cut off, they do so. At least they get one or two office visits out of the people they are scaring into it. It is a planned campaign of terror. They should be prosecuted for criminal activities .(Martin, 1977, <u>Dynamics of Correction of Abnormal Function. Terrence J. Bennett lectures.</u> p.67)*

Within the DNA of each and every cell of our body is a perfect model for a perfect body. DNA has as one of its primary functions to keep the body totally healthy. So how can a disharmonious situation develop within us— why do we get sick? There are two obvious ways for this to happen: either the DNA puts out erroneous information or the perfect pattern gets distorted by the time it is transformed into its end product.

Modern science understands that one way or the DNA to change its information is by the use of retroviruses. These organisms actually go into the nucleus and alter the DNA. One well-known retrovirus is the AIDS virus, which tells the DNA to stop the production of T-cells.

Some people feel that viruses serve a definite function by serving as nature's communication channel. They bring in information from the outside world, and in their own way, they force us to change biophysically. This theory helps to explain how evolution might possibly take place and may be extremely important in our adaptation process. Because of the complexity of viruses, there are currently only two approaches to ridding the body of them. The allopathic method is through immunization. Immunization is the process of inserting a (hopefully) dead virus into the body in order to trick the body into building its defenses against the new enemy. There is much disagreement and discussion as to whether or not this is an effective treatment, because in most cases the diseases were already biologically adapted to and therefore in decline by the time the immunization came into existence. Also, since viruses constantly mutate, there is only a very slim possibility that an identical virus to the immunized one will enter the body, but immunization is a very big business for the pharmaceutical companies and the World Health Organization, so it is the primary methodology currently in place.

The second approach, the vitalistic one, realizes the importance of viruses. For some of us it is hard to look at a small pox epidemic or the black plague of Europe and accept it as a natural process, since thousands of people died, but isn't it really, in hindsight, part of the evolutionary process because the people who survived were stronger for it? We can not judge events such as these as good or bad. However, they could be manifestations of a group consciousness drawing in the endarkenment process: the collective stress of a nation or a sect. The important concept is that if the group consciousness is making choices toward enlightenment, then movements of darkness shouldn't occur.

If DNA is left undisturbed, then the other way that the message gets altered is by closing down the communication channel somewhere between the DNA and its end product, the creation of healthy cells. We talked about this process earlier when we eluded to endarkenment, which in this case is called illness.

One of the vitalistic approaches explaining this process, is illustrated by Sigmund Freud when he wrote,

> *Fixations of the libido may occur at various points in the course of development. If subsequently a repression takes place, the libido flows back to these points (a process called regression), and it is from them that the energy breaks through in the form of a symptom. Later on it became clear that the localization of the point of fixation is what determines the 'choice of neurosis', that is, the form in which the subsequent illness makes its appearance (Strachey, 1968, The Standard Edition of the Complete Works of Sigmund Freud, Vol. XX. p.35).*

Freud was primarily giving a rationale for neurotic behavior, but his quote gives a good explanation for any illness. Depending on where or how we decide to close down will determine our 'illness of choice.'

We can expand this concept further by saying that whenever stress is introduced into our body, the body must somehow compensate for it by adapting. Because stress, by definition, comes as an increase of energy, the adaptation process usually requires that the body either close down some function or wall off the stress from the rest of the body. Hans Selye, a medical doctor and researcher, explains it this way:

> *In its medical sense, stress is essentially the rate of wear and tear in the body. Anyone who feels that whatever he is doing—or whatever is being done to him—is strenuous and wearing, knows vaguely what we mean by stress. The feelings of just being tired, jittery, or ill are subjective sensations of stress. But stress does not necessarily imply a morbid change: normal life, especially intense pleasure and the ecstasy of fulfillment, also cause some wear and tear in the machinery of the body. Indeed, stress can even have curative value, as in shock therapy, bloodletting, and sports. In any event, wear and tear is only the result of all this; hence now we define stress as the nonspecific response of the body to any demand.*

> *...It was found, some forty years ago, that stress causes certain changes in the structure and chemical composition of the body which can be accurately appraised. Some of these changes are merely signs of damage; others are manifestations of the body's adaptive reactions, its mechanism of defense against stress. The totality of these changes- the stress syndrome- is called the general adaptation syndrome (G.A.S.). It develops in three stages: (1) the alarm reaction, (2) the stage of resistance; (3) the stage of exhaustion (Selye, The Stress of Life. 1956, p.1).*

One example of this is when we hit our thumb with a hammer and it swells up. The swelling process isolates that part of our body from the rest. Another example is the flight or fight response. In this response, the sympathetic nervous system channels all the bodily energy to the arms, legs, brain, eyes, and heart, while at the same time, it shuts off the gastrointestinal tract. With this in mind, we can see how someone who lives with a sense of constant flight or fight may end up with gastrointestinal problems, i.e., ulcers, colitis, cystitis, constipation, or stomach cancer, because they live in a state where the energy to this area of their body is shut off or at least diminished. This brings up an interesting question: since stomach cells regenerate themselves every eight hours, how can an ulcer possibly exist longer than eight hours? In other words, the DNA says that within every eight hours I am going to produce a brand new, perfect stomach, yet the hole persists. How does this happen without something or some thought that maintains the position that a hole in the stomach actually is necessary to our well-being?

According to current theories, the body goes through three phases when injured. McCaldy and Willis in their book, <u>Managing Low Back Pain</u>, feel that spinal injuries present first with some sort of <u>dysfunction</u>. This dysfunction shows generally as a decrease in a person's ranges of motion. Then after a period of time without treatment, or wrong treatment, the body will become <u>unstable</u>. Finally the body becomes <u>stable</u> as the body adapts itself to the injury and alters its functions to compensate for the problem.

Many years before Kirkaldy-Willis, Terrance Bennett said it a little differently:

Pathological states like physiology are a chain reaction starting with dysfunction and ending with a pathology that can not be reversed (with) destruction of the tissue (Martin, <u>Dynamics of Correction of Abnormal Function. Terrence J. Bennett lectures</u>. 1977).

Many health professionals deem it important to identify where stress comes from, they break it down into two categories: stress from an outside source like a car accident, lifting the wrong way, or even an abusive parent, or stress from an inside source like fatigue, worry, nutritional imbalance, or a bacterium. Like the old clique says, if we have a hammer, then the whole world is a nail. Likewise, with most medical professionals, a specific stress can usually be found to justify the use of their specialized hammer. For instance, a psychiatrist interviewing a person who was just involved in a car accident might try to prove that the accident happened because of a problem in the anal stage of development. But in basic terms, stress, no matter from what source, turns on some reflexive juices in our body. At the same time , it shuts down others, which either moves us toward our designated goal or creates dysfunction within our body if we don't cope with the increased energy.

Stress is nothing more than information. It allows us to respond to our world as we perceive it, forcing us into action. Most of our stress drives us to action. It is created in our bodies and comes from irrational perceptions of how we should BE in this world. This concept of who we are is stored in the cells of our body and when necessary for our functioning, it is released. From a physiology point of view let's see how this happens:

A nerve cell has two primary purposes: one is to transmit a signal either away from or to the brain or another nerve cell, and the second is to remember a previous action. We usually think that the brain houses all of our memories, but in fact, memory is stored in every nerve cell. So we have memory in the brain, the brain stem, the spinal cord, and in the sympathetic/parasympathetic ganglion on the outside of the spinal cord. Plus, thanks to the new field of psychoimmunology, we now know that things like white blood cells also have a memory.

Starting in the early 1980s, receptors for neurotransmitters and neuropeptides were discovered on cells in the immune system called monocytes, 'Brain' receptors on white blood cells in the blood? It would be hard to exaggerate the significance of this discovery. In the past, it was thought that the central nervous system alone relayed messages to the body, rather like a complicated telephone system connecting the brain to all the organs it wanted to 'talk' to. In this scheme, the neurons function like telephone lines conveying the brain's signals-that is their unique function, shared by no other system in the physiology.

Now it was seen that the brain does not just send impulses traveling in straight lines down the axons, or trunks, of the neurons; it freely circulates intelligence throughout the body's entire inner space (Chopra, Quantum Healing. 1989, p.66).

What does all of this mean?

> *The field of neuropsychology has reached a point where it can assert that everything beings can perceive, conceive, or do is a result of the central nervous system's ability to structure and restructure its own activity (Globus, Consciousness of the Brain. 1976, p.7).*

If we are faced with an event that we perceive relates to our survival, and we learn that a certain response seems appropriate, then our nervous system remembers both the stimulus and the response. If it happens enough, it can literally get hardwired in to us as a permanent way of being in the world. For example, let's say one of our parents was abusive to us when we were a child and we responded by raising our right arm to cover our face. This then becomes our reflex, given any event we perceive to be similar. If we face life by being cautious of everyone around us, then we will find on a physical level that the muscles of our right shoulder are in a state of constant contraction. I have used this as an example because it is a problem I have seen many times in my clinic. In those cases there is usually a relationship between abuse and chronic shoulder/upper back pain. Even though the abusive parent isn't around anymore, the response is hardwired into these patients' bodies. Most of them have had this reflex in operation for so many years that they have reached the stable phase meaning that their body has already adapted. This implies that much therapy will be needed to reverse their process. The first step is to identify both to the health care provider and the patient that this current behavior stems from an irrational perception, then the body can be reconditioned. Trying to fix the body first is a more difficult process, because the body thinks it still needs this pattern for protection.

Robert Becker, a medical researcher and MD, has performed vitalistic research relating to the body's electrical currents and associated electromagnetic forces.

> *Since every reaction and thought seems to produce an evoked potential, the DC (direct current) system seems directly involved in every phase of mental activity. At the very least, the electric sheath acts as a bias control, a sort of background stabilizer that keeps the nerve impulses flowing in the proper direction and regulates their speed and frequency. (Becker, The Body Electric. 1985, p.241)*

It is my belief that healers have been using "electromagnetic therapy" for years. When a healer enters into the electromagnetic realm of another person with the intent of getting to the cause of the person's problem, usually either the healer, the patient, or both will intuitively see or feel the incident which caused the initial stress. Once this is exposed the healing process can begin.

In our clinic, we have found that we can relieve a person of "dis-stress" by working with the electrical fields associated with the somatovisceral reflexes (a point on the skin that causes a reflex in an organ), which is a technique discovered by Terrance Bennett, D.C. According to Bennett's theory, if an organ is in a state of dysfunction it can be identified by these reflexes and a cure can be initiated, providing it has not progressed to a state of pathology. This represents a better course of action, because almost all of our stress has housed within it a flight or fight response and, therefore, shuts down the abdominal areas first. By working to restore the autonomic nervous reflex to the abdomen area, we have found that people also were able to rid themselves of such things as migraines, sciatica, and neck pain. They also were able to develop and maintain inner peace.

Hans Selye, M.D., in his book <u>The Stress of Life</u>, says these are some of the signs that we are not coping with the stress in our lives:

Irritability
Depression
Pounding heart
Dry throat or mouth
Impulsive behavior
Urges to cry or run away
Emotional instability
Inability to concentrate
Dizziness
Fatigue
Anxiety
Being "keyed up"
Nervous tics
Easily startled
Nervous laughter
Stuttering
Teeth clenching
Insomnia
Restlessness
Sweating
Frequent need to urinate
Diarrhea
Constipation
Indigestion
Pain in the neck
Pain in the lower back
Loss of appetite or excessive eating
Increased smoking
Increased use of legal drugs
Alcohol and drug addiction
Nightmares
Neurotic behavior
Psychosis
Accident proneness

To return to our initial questions regarding a definition of a "state of health," we need to see that health is a process. A person never gets sick and is never well, those are judgments that surround our process. A person can be healthy and die of a heart attack, or a person can be sick their whole life and live to a hundred. I admit it is very difficult to look at a four-year-old with muscular dystrophy and not feel sad because he or she is so sick. But the only way he or she can possibly be helped is by understanding that his or her muscular dystrophy is a process, and as a process it can be changed. As a disease, however, there is very little hope for a cure according to the medical model. Fred Wolf, in his book Quantum Body, says this:

> There is no single material cause of cancer, atherosclerosis, osteoarthritis, diabetes, emphysema, or cirrhosis, and in my view, looking for cures, in the conventional sense, is foredoomed. This cause may be consciousness acting through a quantum physical observer effect. (Wolf, Quantum Body. 1986, p.246)

It was Socrates who said, "Know thyself." This is an important concept in this ring, and it implies the need to know more than just our motivations and goals. It also implies the need to know our anatomy and physiology. What makes our bodies work? How can enlightenment be achieved if we remain in the dark?

Likewise, other questions must be addressed that will define what survival means to us as an individual, i.e., do I really need a new car to survive? Once we truly understand that we will survive in any given situation, that stress will leave us as the fear leaves. Is stress, then, our hidden enemy? Do we need to avoid stress at all costs? The answer is no. We need stress in our lives, it is what makes us move. The setting of a goal is stressful, having to go to the bathroom is stressful ( more so for some people), and to some, looking in the mirror is stressful. The master uses the stress that comes into his or her life to find out more about himself or herself. They carefully examine how they react and cope with it.

Many people, it seems, go out of their way to create stress in their lives so they will have a "new" challenge. Science is now showing that these people are probably "adrenaline junkies." They live off of the "high" that adrenaline produces as it rushes through their bodies in response to a new stress. People who fall into this category are found in every walk of life, but they all have one thing in common and that is their desire to change something. For example, they might be the early pioneers, entrepreneurs, revolutionists, substance abusers, or thieves.

To insure an ultimate high, all of these people need to put their survival on the line. The greater the risk, the higher the high. Again, anything done to excess takes us down the path of endarkenment, and so it is with these people who thrive on being "high."

The issue of health has many different facets to it. We find runners who run until it feels like their lungs are going to burst, weight lifters who use corticosteroids (knowing that it will probably kill them), anorexics, bulimics, thousands of dieters, and the list goes on. All of these situations relate to an individual's perception of health verses survival, thereby creating stress. The ability to deal with stress both physically and mentally is what separates the athletic stars from the weekend warriors. How we cope with stress can take us to enlightenment and freedom.

## One More Mile

"One more mile, one more mile," Bill muttered to himself every time his foot struck the ground. He loved to push his body to the limit when he went for his morning run. Today he knew he was going to run the furthest he ever had before. One more mile and he would set a new record for himself.

"I can do it," he said to himself. "Just put one foot in front of the other." He was so focused on his run he didn't know where he was, let alone that there were dark clouds forming overhead.

It was just three years ago that Bill had started to run, it was on his thirtieth birthday. He had visited his doctor for his ten-year physical and the doctor had warned him that unless he did some sort of exercise he would end up in the hospital.

Bill didn't know he would fall in love with running, but it turned out to be the only thing that made any sense in his life. In fact, instead of working sixteen hours a day always trying to get one more sale like he used to, now he was working three or four hours a day and some days he didn't even show up. So Bill knew that running was helping him, because workaholics don't live very long. No one understood Bill, not his boss, his parents, nor his family.

Because of his constant running, Bill was able to see things more clearly. He now understood that he had a miserable home life because all his family wanted from him was his money. They didn't care about his health or they would be more supportive of his new activity. He used to think his family problems were because he had to work so much, but now, because his income was much smaller, he could see that they were unhappy because of their greed. His family always wanted one more thing.

"One more mile" had become Bill's slogan. He was truly free while running; there were no pressures from the outside world. His only limitation was his body, but he knew if he asked it to do one more mile, it would respond. He loved the feeling when his heart pounded so hard it would echo on the adjoining hills. Not only his heart, but he also loved the pain in his legs and feet. Running was Bill's ultimate high.

Bill was just rounding his final corner and heading up a long, steep hill toward his new personal record, when the clouds opened up and it started to pour. The sudden rain quickly turned the path to mud and Bill, still focused on the hill ahead and achieving his personal best, slipped, falling into the ravine that bordered his last mile, where he died.

This story has a great moral: There is always one more ultimate high, if that is what you are looking for.

I have attempted to show that a person's state of health is an individualistic perception of what makes them feel good, and it is directly related to how they cope with their world in both the present and the past . All too often, as with the runner in the story, feeling good about our health is directly caused by an adrenaline rush. These people subconsciously associate perfect health with the high produced by adrenaline. Therefore, a perfect state of health can be defined as being able to physically, emotionally, and intellectually cope with any past, present, or future stress.

The way to cope with stress is through body awareness by understanding physiology and anatomy and avoiding excesses. Excess implies loss of control and personal responsibility, realizing that the hard-wiring which occurred is OUR response to a stressful situation. Thus, we try to understand the connectiveness of body, mind, and spirit.

Yes, within this ring are contained many wonderful adventures. Mastery of the Survival Ring games are the most difficult , because the rules are so different. Many people try to master the other rings first, but without mastery of the Physical Ring, they find little point of reference and usually end up becoming very frustrated. Once mastery is accomplished on this level, then the games can be applied to the other rings and be more fun and fulfilling.

Another example of a minor pretend game within this ring is the game of money. Money doesn't have the black and white implications of health, but it is important because it has caused the death of many people through wars, suicides, and murders. Money in itself can not kill us or take us to immortality, but it can, it seems, buy better medical care and an easier life.

I once asked a fairly well-to-do friend of mine the metaphysical secret to making a lot of money. He said that if we were to look at who had the majority of money in this country, we would find that it would be the crime syndicates. Therefore, money really has nothing to do with any high or lofty principles. So I asked another friend of mine the secret of making money, and he responded, "it is very simply, real estate." What he was saying was that he got lucky in a particular game that earned him some money and therefore the thought that it was the ultimate answer. However, I have known as many people who went broke in real estate as have made money (he later went bankrupt). How many times have we asked God for more money? In actuality, there is enough money in this country for every person to be a multimillionaire.

At a sales seminar once, I heard a great answer on how to become a millionaire. The speaker said, "It's easy; all we need to do is make more than we spend." And, in fact, I have always sensed he was right, although I, like most of us, find it difficult to do.

We must again remember that the wealthy are not any more enlightened than the poor. They are just playing the same game with a different focus and achieving different rewards. The poor person, like the new moon, is pretending to be closed down, and the wealthy person, like the full moon, is pretending to be open. Generally, the poor person is playing mostly by himself, while the wealthy person is playing with many others. Within the Survival Ring, the wealthy person dreams of simplifying his life like the poor person, and the poor person dreams of becoming rich. We always seem to have this contrast ever-present. The only thing that is different between the two is their thought process and where they choose to focus their attention. The games of the poor are as much fun as those of the rich, and either one can give us our "ultimate highs."

The poor person gets to complain to all his friends about how bad things are because he can't pay his rent, or utility bills, or whatever. In this country, a person is allowed to become a ward of the state by receiving welfare and getting to face the humility of that whole situation. These may sound like dismal games, but we should not judge them. In many cases, this is a way of proving to themselves that someone else loves them (the old pretending not to be loved game). On the positive side, they are proving to themselves that they can receive money with little or no effort, although in many cases the dollar per hour rate is pretty small: they can spend weeks trying to manipulate the system or each other for a mere fifty dollars. Even so, they perceive this as receiving money without working which gives them a feeling of freedom.

The wealthy person, on the other hand, gets to worry about keeping all his money and gets to complain about all the poor people who are after it. In many cases, he gets to pretend that he became rich because he is a superior person. Many became rich because of the sacrifice made on the part of the poor people. The poor person, because he is choosing to be poor, must actually give his share of the money to the rich, thereby allowing the poor person to play the poor game and the rich person to play the rich game. Because of this agreement, both get to experience the life they have chosen.

To add another variation: some poor people set the game up so that they can rise from poverty to wealth, while some rich people go from wealth to poverty. Both are easy to play when the rules are established, albeit, going from wealth to poverty is usually a little faster. We as a society criticize the use of illegal drugs, but drugs more than anything else create these transitions: consider the wealthy person who uses drugs and loses everything and the poor person who becomes rich by dealing drugs. As with all the rings, once we experience both sides of the coin, the rules become more apparent. This is one of our goals.

One focus of the poor requires that they pretend that money is limited; we find many poor people who hold onto whatever they have with clenched fists. They pretend that this is all they will ever get. Most remain poor because they will still indulge themselves, but very seldom will they give into family and friend's requests for money. They are able to confirm their belief in a limited money supply, because their actions shut off the flow of money to them. A flow requires an input as well as an output. If the output is shutdown, the flow becomes a stagnant pool.

A person falls into the poor category if he or she feels he or she needs more money, which means some wealthy people fall into this category as well those at the poverty level. If that feeling exists, he or she is playing the limited money game. As with our health, if we have stress around money then something must close down to compensate for the added energy. The Tao explains the proper way to relieve all of this stress when it says "enough is always enough."

As in all games, there are many variations. But primarily the way to wealth is to create a fantasy that is so good people will want to pay for the opportunity of playing. The real wealthy also understand the premise that the number of people who play is directly proportional to the amount of money received. So the best fantasies are the ones aimed at the people who are spending more than they are earning and want to change that by becoming rich with very little effort. So, we have invented things like stock corporations, insurance, drugs, fraud, and all of the other get rich quick schemes that allow us the chance to become rich with very little effort on our part.

There are many ways to create a fantasy, but the primary ingredient is to offer other people something they don't have or think they need more of. Whether it be salvation, more money, more sex, or more knowledge, they first must believe that they do not have enough. For instance, the people who are currently working for minimum wage in this country have bought into someone else's fantasy. The fantasy is based on a belief that someone else, the company, must provide some sort of security for them, or they bought into the overall national fantasy that they are just pawns in the big chess game and don't have a right to play or aren't smart enough to play. No matter what we are currently doing, it is a result of either us buying into someone else's fantasy, them buying into ours, or a compromise.

If a person is a factory worker and decides they want to earn more money, they could do it by changing jobs, i.e., moving up the ladder. To do this, they would need to get management to participate in one of their fantasies—that only with help can they have more than they currently have. Most managers subconsciously understand this game and therefore try to surround themselves with people who will support their belief that they deserve to be the manager. So, to move into the manager's organization, the worker would have to first show that he or she could fit into the manager's fantasy without disrupting it, and second, that he or she could help the manager justify his fantasy to the manager's bosses.

In reality, then, what is the difference between the president of a company and the janitor, besides their income? Basically, the janitor is living out his fantasy with the head custodian, and the president is living his with the board of directors. Both are playing in someone else's game and both are also playing their own game by making their "boss" think they are important. So, apparently, the real difference in income happens when we decide who we are going to play with. Our environment and who we play with, become all important.

To change a game generally requires that first we change our environment. It is extremely difficult to play the game of wealth when surrounded by poor people. The primary reason for this is our inability to learn the new game rules with old game players. If we decide we want to be a president of a company, then we need to find someone who can teach us how to play that game, if not by practical how-to knowledge, then at least by being a model. The only real difference is how these people define their fantasy. By extending their focus to playing with lots of money, they eventually believe they deserve to have it, and therefore it comes. If we just dream of the day that we will become a president of a company, it will never happen. However, if we focus on our dream and build a foundation under it, as Thoreau said, then our dream will manifest. We must become indispensable.

In the case of the janitor, building a foundation under his dream to be president could mean first moving into the head custodian position. Then moving into his new boss's position, and on up. It might also require that he attend school or some other activity to get the knowledge he needs to make the transitions. This is where the trouble comes in, most of us don't want to do the things necessary to play the games we have dreamed about. We would rather pretend we can play someone else's game by our rules. (I had a friend once who wanted to be a psychologist, but instead of going to school to learn the rules, he ordered a five dollar mail-order minister's degree and did "spiritual counseling." He never could understand why he didn't feel successful in his life.) If our boss thinks we are going to invoke rule changes in the current game, an advancement opportunity will never arise and the dream will always remain a dream. Mastery only comes by learning the existing rules. New rules can not be made and accepted by others until we have proved to them that we have mastered the existing ones.

To help us understand what our current game is, we must only look around at the other people in our environment. In metaphysics we call this the reflective process. Whatever we see in the people around us is a direct reflection of where we are. We can spend eons looking at all of the reflections we see of ourselves and analyzing them, but really the only service it performs is to show us what games we are playing and why we are stuck in games we don't really want to play. The way out is always to change our environment. In other words, make a conscious decision to not play with these people anymore and find some new players.

Within the Survival Ring we find that in one way or another all of our games allow us to focus on one or more of our survival needs. These needs are food, clothing, shelter, or rest. If we decide to play the wealth game, we do it so that we may upgrade things in these four areas. Once the rules to the Survival Ring are experienced, we understand that in some way these four things are always provided. It may not be up to our expectations, but they are always provided. We may live in a flophouse, eat beans, shop at Goodwill, and sleep on the floor, but at least we are being provided the necessities of life. So anything we want beyond these basics requires better game playing, and once we believe that those necessities will always be provided, we then understand the lower limit to the game. Understanding the lower limit helps us become detached from the game itself. Fear or ignorance, instead of understanding of the lower limit, ties us into the game and makes us pawns.

Again, we are in the only Heaven where these four items are of any significance. So the games we play with these four items are unique, complex, and extremely fun. Most of the activities related to food, clothing, shelter, and rest are ones that help us justify our separation from God and/or society.

People on this level use the word "poor" as a motivation to do something. If they have poor eating habits, they become vegetarians, fast, take vitamins, and so on. If they have poor clothing, they go on a buying spree, trying to become more in fashion. If they have poor shelter, they may lease-purchase a home or buy a home. If they have poor rest, they may learn meditation or altered dream states.

Another unique game on this level is the one that encompasses relationships. On this level, most relationships have as their base a physical experience, and most revolve around sex, primarily as a physical gratification experience: a physical climax or as a way to create something physical—a baby. Many of these relationships fall apart because of their own shallowness. After all, how many times can we experience the same exact physical game without it becoming boring?

Since one of the primary elements of this level is activity, most relationships exist primarily so that we may have another to play with. For instance, if we like to dance, we will undoubtedly find a partner who also likes to dance; if we like to drink, we will find a drinking buddy; if we like to go to church, then we will meet someone in church. When we tire of that activity, simultaneously we tire of our partner. We then look for another activity and another partner. Our focus is generally on the activity and not on how we are playing within that activity or who we are playing with.

One of the key words to this level is the word "effort." On this level, if we are playing hard in our activity, we will find that it takes much effort on our part. So we find people who are workaholics, climb high mountains, fast for weeks, etc. at the one extreme and on the other, people who watch television twelve hours a day, eat out all the time, do no exercise, etc. The contrast is maximum effort verses minimum effort within the realm of physical activity. The primary fable is that we need to work hard to make anything of ourselves. Until we master this level, this will remain a predominant belief.

In summation, the Survival Ring is the densest of all the Rings and enables the members of this Heaven to experience extremes of the greatest variation. This is the only Ring that involves a life and death struggle and that uses money as a product of substance. We pretend that we are alive and that we will eventually experience death. Many of our activities are designed to further entrench us in this feeling of aliveness. These include adrenaline rushes, sexual rushes, fear of death, violence, elation, and successes. The minor pretend games of this Ring are numerous but all feed into our belief that we are alive.

Being alive is not the opposite of dying. Rather, the opposite is immortality—living forever. This is a concept that has been somehow removed from this Ring. Many people look death in the face every day, but very few even admit the possibility of immortality. The problem comes from our linear thinking which teaches that entropy—everything is always moving toward disorder—is true. Entropy implies that the only possible end result for man, woman, animals, plants, the planet, or the universe is death.

The opposite of entropy is order or what some term as syntropy—things tend to reach higher levels of organization, order, and dynamic harmony. Albert Szent-Gyoergyi, the Nobel Prize winning biologist, refers to it as an innate drive in living matter to perfect itself. Order is created by increasing energy to a system, a process I call "enlightenment." Enlightenment for the participants of the Survival Ring manifests when their perception of all the minor pretend games focuses on and includes immortality, at least as an option.

Freedom from life and death struggles no longer exists for the immortal person.

*Knowing others is wisdom;*
*Knowing the self is enlightenment.*
*Mastering others requires force;*
*Mastering the self needs strength.*

*He who knows he has enough is rich.*
*Perseverance is a sign of will power.*
*He who stays where he is endures.*
*To do but not to perish is to be eternally present.*
        *—The Tao translated by Gia-Fu Feng and Jane English*

# Chapter 6
## Mental Ring (Second Heaven)

Once we are aware of our daily routines, our dreams, and have a desire to change our actions with regard to the Survival Ring, then we need to move to the next step: developing a means to an end, a plan. This is accomplished by changing our focus to the Mental Ring level.

This level is a support function to our actions of the Survival Ring level in that it allows us to do more than reflex-motivated activities. It allows us to pretend to have control over our actions, to premeditate movements, and to weigh the results of our actions.

Whereas our actions in Survival Ring are for the most part linear, with the addition of the Mental Ring we can now create actions in two dimensions. An example of this is a person working on an assembly line. He does the job he was told to do without variation, otherwise the end product would be different from what was intended. Compare this activity to the artist who thinks while he or she is painting; his end product will be different every time because he has added another variable, his mind.

Housed within this level we find a wide range of participants which vary from those who just think about what they are doing, finding the best way to get from point A to point B on one extreme, to the group who consider themselves "intellectuals" at the other extreme.

The "electron ring" representing this level goes through the Throat Chakra and the solar plexus in classical Chakra terms. The main function of this ring is to teach us expression. When we focus on the lower part of the ring, we try to use knowledge to help us express ourselves in physical ways. When we focus on the upper part of the ring, we try to express ourselves in spiritual ways. When we understand the contrasts of the games within this ring, we express ourselves in everything we do.

While power is generally expressed in physical terms at the Survival Ring level (physically stronger or more cunning), within the Mental level it is represented by knowledge. The more knowledge we can accumulate, the more powerful we think we are. But this is a misnomer, it is not the knowledge as much as the ability to express what we know. Those who are able to express themselves are the ones who receive the Nobel Prizes, for example. Any researcher will readily admit that the research is the easiest part, the hard part comes in writing the grant to back the project, explaining the research, and finally, trying to find a journal willing to publish the information.

Max Plank said:

> *An important scientific innovation rarely makes its way by gradually winning over and converting its opponents: it rarely happens that Saul becomes Paul. What does happen is that its opponents gradually die out and that the growing generation is familiarized with the idea from the beginning.(Becker, The Body Electric: Electromagnetism and the Foundation of Life. 1985, p.330)*

For intellectuals, the physical world transforms from all of the hustle and bustle of the Survival Ring level to become a classroom for experiment and study for the purpose of explaining the activities we do. This requires constant observation of the physical world and then the assimilation of those observations into theories. These theories are then usually given to someone in the Survival Ring games to justify, because they are the doers.

The premise of this level is that we are all ignorant of the laws comprising this universe or of the other heavens. We try to put all the rules of any Survival Ring activity into analytical form. A good example is this book, which assumes that no one understands the model. Therefore, I am trying to explain it in an analytical form. In reality, everyone already understands everything in this book, but in some cases they are pretending not to.

If we were to watch someone on this level, we would see that they had no real concern with basic survival needs. A scientist could lock himself or herself in his or her lab for days without eating, sleeping, or, yes, even wearing clothes. Attaining knowledge is all that is important, motivated by the thought that he or she will find a breakthrough that will throw new light on an existing game.

The research process is rather complex because first it requires an unusual observation, like an apple falling out of a tree, then serious contemplation on the observation, as we try to formulate a substantial question, since knowledge can not be uncovered without the proper question. Once a decent question is raised, then a hypothesis can be deduced, followed by more observation to see if there could eventually be justification which will lead to the formulation of a theory.

An interesting phenomena happens to most of these theories, they stay around for a few years and the scientific community marvels at the wisdom of the theory, and then eventually proves it to be invalid or incomplete. With the understanding of quantum physics, this situation is finally being understood, because we now know that the observer, by being a part of his own experiment, alters the outcome. In other words, the scientist is creating a new game with a new application of the rules. Those other scientists who want to play the new game and play by the newly established rules will be impressed by the brilliance of this scientist. However, when another looks at the game and sees the existing rules and alters one of them, the game changes and the information derived from the experiment no longer fits into the box created by the first scientist. On the surface, it may appear to be the same game, but it is not.

As an example, if we were to take a beaker of water and analyze it, we would find all the components that the scientific community tells us comprises water: two parts hydrogen and one part oxygen. But if a spiritual master touched the beaker and the contents turned to wine, how could we ever justify that within the present scientific model? Would it go down in history that we were ignorant and our box that defined water was in error? Or would we assume that it was a fluke of nature or a miracle and let it go at that? Would we assume that the Master had changed the rules on us and proceed to try to understand the new rules?

One of the major obstacles in this Ring is we have a tendency to lock ourselves into certain boxes. We tend to believe that if a person is able to justify a theory, then it must be correct. We forget that knowledge is fluid, and as such, what is accepted as fact today may be wrong tomorrow. If knowledge was fixed, then the people playing within this Ring would soon run out of games to play. David Bohm, a quantum physicist, said, *The universe will never be explained, but scientists will have the pleasure of winding round and about never-endingly into it (Briggs, <u>Looking Glass Universe: The Emerging Science of Wholeness. 1984</u>, p.121).*

Whereas the scientific community uses analytics to justify their theories, the philosophers use assumptions. Philosophy is the process of either seeing ourselves through the eyes of the world, or seeing the rest of the world through ourselves. A sound philosophy implies finding an all encompassing theory that explains everything in the universe. Like, for instance, this book's philosophy that we are on a recreational planet and therefore we are here to play. It is an all encompassing philosophy explaining human behavior and man's existence on earth. Philosophy must be based on assumption, because the premises can never be proved until such time as scientific knowledge derives a process of measuring that allows an analytical interpretation of the assumption. For instance the assumption posed by Einstein that the universe is expanding could not be proven until science had developed the radio telescope.

Most breakthroughs in the scientific community come because of a major realigning of philosophy or a paradigm shift. Many of the people who have contributed greatly to science were considered, in their time, to be philosophers. Whatever title we wish to label someone—a philosopher or scientist—still implies they are playing within the Mental Ring games.

Neither philosophy nor scientific theories do mankind any good at all if they are kept on this level. If these theories cannot be applied in a useful productive manner, they remain just a mental exercise. Therefore, part of the game on this level is to be able to apply these theories within the games of Survival Ring.

We do find that within the Mental Ring there are many dissertations providing great mental stimulation to this level's participants. We can also find many people who sound very intelligent, who appear to have all the answers, but they are doing nothing to experience life. Many of these choose this level thinking they can escape from the experiences of Survival Ring, only to wake up some day wondering what happened to their life.

This is not a level of escape as some people think. It is a level for acquiring knowledge so that the games of Survival Ring are more enjoyable.

The basic pretend games are, at the extremes, knowledge verses ignorance. But one of the more subtler games represents the contrasts within the known versus the unknown of the physical world. Pretending that there is knowledge available to us that has not yet been uncovered is a great motivation to those wishing to play this intellectual game. They may find that current knowledge is very boring, and therefore reach for the excitement of the unknown. Also, with the discovery of some facet of the unknown comes prestige, fame, and recognition. The discoverer is called brilliant and given numerous rewards, sometimes. However, if they did not follow the proscribed rules and methods to acquire their new knowledge, they are ridiculed and despised.

Another of the games is the one called "student-teacher." This game requires that one person pretends to have information currently unavailable to the others. Then he establishes schools whereby he can transmit this information. This game allows the students to fulfill their fantasies of being ignorant and allows the teachers their fantasies of being powerful because of their knowledge. One of the problems with this game is if one of the students asks the right question to the teacher, then inherently the teacher can realize his own ignorance and the student can realize his own knowledge. If this happens, the game might be destroyed.

Of course, as mentioned earlier, most of these games are devised for poor people so they may have the opportunity to give away their money. In this case, they get to buy power through the acquisition of knowledge.

Usually once a little bit of knowledge is acquired, most players let it go to their head and develop a feeling that they are smarter than everyone else. It becomes truly a level of arrogance. They go out into the world and, because of their brilliance, they think they have control over every aspect of life. Part of this comes because they learn how easy it is to manipulate those people within the Survival Ring level. It becomes rather easy to present an argument verifying their position, and the people within Survival Ring let them do whatever they want. However, because being smarter is only a pretend game, those that try to manipulate others usually end up getting manipulated themselves.

There are many people who are representative of this level, but one of the best is a fictional character, Sherlock Holmes. Sherlock had the philosophy that he did not want any knowledge unless it directly pertained to crime fighting. He would spend hours and hours developing crime fighting tools and philosophies. If anyone tried to tell him non-related information, he would quickly dismiss it as triviality. He also was in pursuit of an unknown nemesis—a master criminal, which drove him to excellence in his field of crime fighting.

One of the keys to success at this level is to become specific in the knowledge we acquire. General knowledge only lets us play generalized games with minor intensity. Specific knowledge allows us to play specific games and increases the intensity, thereby allowing greater rewards.

Most knowledge games are structured so that the players must go through different levels to acquire it. These can be called the "generalist-specialist" games. Whenever we decide to start acquiring knowledge, we generally must start at a broad all-encompassing level. Within this level, we can look at all the knowledge currently available on the subject. We acquire a generalized approach to this set of knowledge. As we study the generalized material, we can generally find one specific item that really strikes our fancy.

As we delve into that one area, we become a specialist. We learn to focus our attention on just that one idea or concept, trying to learn everything about it. However, once we start to understand this new concept, we find that it actually opens up into another broad world—automatically, we become a generalist again.

Then as we explore this new world, we will find another single concept that again strikes our fancy. So as we move into that, we again become a specialist. Thus, the whole process goes on and on. For example, let's create a person who decides to go to college. He goes through the first two years as a generalist, studying a wide range of subjects. As he approaches his junior year, he decides on a major and chooses philosophy; he is now a specialist. As he enters the realm of philosophy, he sees that he has many philosophical avenues to pursue, so again he is a generalist. He picks a particular branch of metaphysics to study, which moves him back into a specialty. Once he starts studying metaphysics, he again sees many different philosophical avenues to pursue, so he is a generalist again., etc.

Because we seem to have a national belief that we are better off remaining "jack-of-all-trades," we may find we have a great reluctance to moving into a specialty. This fear comes from believing that by becoming too specialized, we may end up starving to death. Having that fear implies the possibility, but the reality of it seldom exists. People who are vigorous game players try to move into a specialty whenever they find one. The specialist game is one of the most fun and exciting ones on this level, and one of the primary ways to grow intellectually.

Relationships existing between people on this level are usually formulated intellectually with one of the partners pretending to be smarter than the other one and constantly offering to teach his or her perceived inferior.

However, the perfect marriage relationship within Mental Ring is one where neither is the teacher nor student, but where each takes intellectual knowledge and together they apply it to the physical activities offered by Survival Ring. They actively participate in the Survival Ring classroom together formulating a philosophy that is uniquely theirs. This philosophy is derived from mutual observations of the world. Once their philosophy is formulated, they both simultaneously apply that philosophy, as they experience the games of the Survival Ring. Ideally, their philosophy should be interpreted as fluid thought and not cast in stone with periodical evaluations to see whether it still has any validity or whether it is time to throw it away and start all over.

Within any philosophical argument there needs to be experiences of the inherent contrasts. These contrasts should be eagerly undertaken by both partners and explored to their limits. After each exploration, the philosophical argument should be updated with their new findings.

We find under this type of arrangement that as long as the philosophy is sound and updated, the marriage will remain solid. If the philosophy proves to be invalid for one of the marriage partners, often the marriage will be destroyed.

It should also be noted that, because this is an expressive level, this is where we find most of the artistic community. The artist tries to put his or her visions or knowledge into artistic form. A musician may hear music in everything he or she observes and try to compose music around that; the painter tries to express the beauty he or she sees in the world; and the writer tries to put his or her visions or knowledge into words. As with all games, it is far more important to just enjoy the activity than to worry about the results. Just by putting their ideas into physical form is to bring those into concepts into the Survival Ring realms. The better they are in their expression, the better they will be received by others. Those artists who become results-oriented usually end up transforming their expression into just another money game, and their expression becomes distorted.

This level is important because it is the first level that allows us to change. Change requires an intellectual feed-back system supported by an educated mind. Without some sort of education, be it listening to others, reading, or acquiring an advanced degree, change can never be implemented. A formal or informal education allows us to be a multidimensional person and greatly increases our ability to express what we know.

Stress on this level is easily detected because of the obvious physical manifestations. Fears around not living up to the expectations of others, like doing a job that the person feels he or she is not qualified to do, will cause stomach or upper abdominal symptoms. Fears of not standing up for what a person believes is right will cause throat problems. Both are problems of expression. These fears extend to areas other than work, like the wife or husband who believes they are not living up to the expectations of their spouse; or the person who is afraid they will be ridiculed every time they open their mouth.

The two Chakras in this ring represent personal power. When we can learn to express ourselves without fear of retribution, then we master this level. This does not mean we should express ourselves arrogantly or flippantly, but rather to know deep inside that we are doing what we need to do for ourselves and that our expression is philosophically sound and grounded in what we perceive as truth. We take our truth and express it in physical form. These physical actions then become very powerful. They become what Chaos Theory terms "attractors." These attractors provide a way to help us and others put our apparent chaos into an order.

*The wise student hears of the Tao and practices it diligently,*
*The average student hears of the Tao and gives it thought now and again.*
*The foolish student hears of the Tao and laughs aloud.*
*If there were no laughter, the Tao would not be what it is.*
*—The Tao translated by Gia-Fu Feng and Jane English*

# Chapter 7
## Ethical Ring (Third Heaven)

Within the Survival Ring, we operate in one dimension, action. When we add the Mental Ring to our actions, we have two dimensions, which include premeditated actions. With the addition of the Ethical Ring we move to a three dimensional space which decreases predictability. The Ethical Ring gives us the ability to differentiate right from wrong in a moral sense, so with the addition of this Ring are able to perform premeditated actions with awareness of consequences.

Reflex actions are pretty much the same for all people in the Survival Ring: we all basically have the same drives and responses to stimuli. Our thought processes are also pretty much the same, but they will vary according to a person's education. However, when we include a person's perception of morality into our model, the Ethical Ring, we see tremendous variation. Morals may be the primary causation that separates us as individuals.

Morality itself is a mixture of a person's culture, societal "norms," religion, and ability to pretend that there will be no consequences for a particular action (the current terminology is "in denial"). This is the branch of philosophy called Ethos (ethics).

Morality can be found by looking at the contrasts between good and evil, i.e., a God versus a Devil. To try to be good implies that we must first pretend we are evil (original sin), and in order to pretend that our God is a good God, we must also pretend that there is an evil God, who we call the Devil.

To experience the Ethical Ring means we must sit in judgment of ourselves in relation to every act we commit and judge it as moral or immoral, according to our philosophy. Generally, we believe that everyone has a set of morals, which allows us to trust our neighbor. However, for people not involved in the Ethical Ring, their set of morals are reflexive in nature—they bend in accordance to a rationalized perception of right and wrong. It is unknown from day-to-day what will be considered right and wrong. In many cases, it is easy to come to the conclusion that people <u>not</u> within this Ring haven't any morals. Of course, this is a wrong assumption. Everyone has morals, but to some they either change radically periodically or they are downplayed in that person's life. Because morals are based on such varied input, it is virtually impossible to find two people with identical ones. That is why one of the first things a newly forming organization must do is develop a code of ethics, so all of their members can accept and operate from somewhat of a consistent basis. A code of ethics takes some of the chaotic behavior out of the group and allows us to trust other members.

Carl Jung says,

> *In practical terms, ...good and evil are no longer self-evident. We have to realize that each represents a judgment... Nevertheless we have to make ethical decisions. The relativity of 'good' and 'evil' by no means signifies that these categories are invalid, or do not exist. (Jung, Memories, Dreams, Reflections, 1963, p.329)*

Immoral acts are often performed in defiance of our own ethics. They can only be performed when we are seeking an adrenaline rush (as already discussed), or as a statement that the moral structure of society does not include the perpetrator. The father or mother who abuses their kids must rationalize that the normal code of ethics does not apply to them or their kids, maybe even to the extent that they "own" their kids and can do with them what they want. The thief rationalizes that he is entitled to someone else's property and, because he has an unfulfilled need, he can then take ownership, regardless.

The process of rationalization can only happen when we accept one singular concept as the whole issue and the needs of the one overshadow all else. This approach allows us to skew the moral codes in place at the time.

The "electron ring" of this Ring circles through the Third Eye Chakra and the Abdominal Chakra in classical terms. This ring is primarily dealing with right action. At one extreme, if we focus at the Abdominal Chakra, we find that right action is constituted around self-fulfillment: the needs of the one outweigh the needs of the many. If we focus our attention at the Third Eye Chakra, we find the other extreme which is right action for the whole: the needs of the many outweigh the needs of the one.

In the countries which practice either Judaism or Christianity, the basic list of moral requirements comes from the Ten Commandments, which comprise a complex code of ethics used by the different religions to help justify their belief systems. A specific religion is defined by its code of ethics: what is right and what is wrong. This allows us the opportunity to play with others in a well-defined moral arena. When someone announces to the world that he is a Christian, he is saying that he is supposedly playing within the Ethical Ring level. When he adds that he is a Fundamentalist and we are Catholic, then we know that we have a different code of ethics; we inherently believe in a different right and wrong.

Our moral fiber comes primarily from our religious beliefs, which are reinforced by some type of spiritual activity with the goal of teaching us to focus on this Ring. Some activities focus us on the Abdominal Chakra, i.e., do something to save our soul. Others focus us on the Third Eye Chakra, i.e., we perform acts that benefit all of mankind.

To help us entrench these ideologies into our everyday actions so they may become a reflex action, we have developed ritual. A ritual is a constant repetition of some dogma or practice. It can be as simple as going to church every Sunday or as complicated as Kundalini Yoga. With all of these rituals comes the promise of enlightenment, if precisely followed, or Hell or endarkenment if performed improperly or not at all.

The people actively pursuing this Ring spend most of their waking hours in concentration on their particular rituals. Good examples of people on this level would be the monks housed in a monastery. They spend all their time following the rituals laid out before them, as they desperately search for God.

The minor pretend games include contemplation, meditation, and prayer; all are ways of communicating with God, and all include some sort of devotional practice. We find that every religious organization has its own set of rituals. Even if they are housed within a central organization like say the Baptists, each church within that organization will have unique rituals. Therein we find the need for so many churches and religions. Each religion and church gets to play its own game. One is not any better than the other, they just simply choose to play different games. We have been given tremendous latitude in terms of which games we chose to play within this Ring. If we decide we don't like a particular church's game, then we can change by simply changing churches.

The primary practice in this Ethical Ring is discipline. Generally it is implied to mean not becoming involved in the Survival Ring games, but really it means to faithfully follow a particular ritual. If we don't follow the ritual as laid out, then the leader has lost power over us, and we are labeled "undisciplined." Therefore, a disciple is someone who dogmatically follows a specific discipline.

We usually think of churches when we talk about religions, but the worship of anything constitutes a religion. So we can find Gods in the form of money, sex, politics, cars, another person, a special book, or any number of things. Once we subconsciously define a God, then we automatically develop a ritual to worship it, him, or her. Many of the activities at the Survival Ring level are rituals in one form or the other.

We can also define God as a man on a throne in Heaven, a Master from another time, someone from another dimension or planet, a special religious book, or something else. No matter what or who we define as God, when we develop a ritual around our concept, we accept that definition as fact and we worship our God as we've defined him or her. Then we recruit others to join us in our specific rituals in order to show the world that we are just like our God, so that we may be accepted as such.

An example would be someone who religiously worships sex. These people live for this activity and treat their sex organs as God, as all there is. In many ways, they respond to their God much like the monks respond to theirs, in that they have developed ritual around it. They spend their waking hours consumed by their God. I even had one person tell me that he was sure every time he climaxed he went through an enlightenment process.

In contrast, we might find a person who is celibate. They may have the inherent feeling that their sex organs are the instrument of the devil and will lead to their demise. Or, usually, celibacy is a ritual requiring the use of denial as a basis for discipline.

When we take our understanding of ritual to the Mental Ring, we develop theology. In theology we analytically define the tenets and activities of the Ethical Ring level. Theology always encompasses the theologians definition of God and the appropriate rituals to reach the objective, whatever that may be. The theologian must inherently believe first that no one is God, all are lost somewhere on the path, and if their definition and activity is not followed, all will end up in some Godforsaken place like Hell.

One of the newer games to come on the scene as of late, is where people approach the Ethical Ring from an analytical, scientific point of view, i.e., Christian Science, Religious Science, etc. These participants think they can analytically discuss the merits of discipline and just by having the knowledge of how it is done, reach the goals of the disciple. When a person has knowledge of the Ethical Ring disciplines but prefers to talk about them instead of applying them, he is said to have a spiritual ego. Having spiritual ego will never make us a Master.

The proper process of the Ethical Ring initiate is to immerse himself or herself in a particular discipline until he or she understands the rules of that discipline. When we know that we know the contrasts, then we must take that knowing and express it as theology. Our next step is then to apply it on the physical level. If a discipline or a theology has no application on the physical level, then it is an invalid discipline. It has been said when the initiate can see the face of God in the toilet he or she is cleaning, then and only then, does he or she understand the principles.

If we pretend that Heaven is someplace other than where we are now, then we must also believe that there is a Hell. As wonderful as we can picture Heaven, then we must also be able to picture a Hell just as awful. There currently are some churches who preach about Heaven and deny that Hell exists. If we believe that our good deeds will take us to Heaven, we must also believe that our bad deeds will take us to Hell. The implication that we must strive to go to Heaven, implies we are by nature headed for Hell.

In reference to the vision at the beginning of this book where God's resting place was called "Heaven," there was no moral decision involving the word "Heaven" as to whether or not it was good or bad. Heaven was just described as a place. Only judgment can call it good or bad.

Let me try to explain this metaphorically with a story called:

## Oh, Rats

There I was surrounded by total filth and obnoxious smells. Rats as big as dogs were running helter-skelter, gorging themselves on last night's dinner. It was always dark and murky, but with all of this, it was still my home.

Both of my parents were killed in the great "Moral War" and I was left to fend for myself. I still hate them for leaving me alone and making me go through this absurdity, but I am resolved to living in this blind alley for the rest of my life.

I admit it is not as nice as the place where I used to live. My mother kept our house very neat and it seemed to always smell of just-baked bread. But at least I can live here in this alley without having to worry about being evicted.

It was one day, only one day, after my parents were killed that the landlord came and kicked me out of my house. I pleaded with him, but he kept saying, "What is right, is right. You can't afford the rent, so you gotta leave."

Sure, I am missing some of the conveniences that I had at home, but I am getting by. I have a special corner in the alley that I can use for a toilet, and I either beg for money or steal my food. Once a week, I walk to the river for my bath. So I have all my needs met. Actually, for only being ten, I think I have things pretty well under control.

I do feel a little guilty when I steal my food, because I was brought up with the belief that stealing was wrong but I don't steal very much, just enough to eat. Besides, what else can I do? I tried to find some work, but a ten-year-old girl with no experience can't do anything to make money.

I can't tell you how much I've learned. I have met other kids in the same boat who have taught me the ropes of the street, and I always remember the words of our landlord, "What is right, is right." I don't want to die, so it is right that I do whatever is necessary to survive, be it stealing, begging, lying, or cheating.

You ask if my actions are moral, and I honestly have to answer you that they must be, since they are right. I do realize that the people I steal from think I am immoral, but that is only because they are selfish. They are just like me; they are stealing from the people who buy their food when they reap excessive profits, so what's the difference? If they opened their hearts to me, I wouldn't have to steal it, right?

All of these were thoughts I had when I was ten. I stayed in that alley for seven years, eking out a survival for myself. When I was seventeen, God intervened for me and gave me a great plan. Because of the war, our country was experiencing a meat shortage. It wasn't something I knew of firsthand, because I could never afford such a luxury. It was then that God gave me the idea to grind up the rats, and sell them as hamburger. I mean they were so big that, by the pound, each rat was worth a fortune. Actually, the catalyst for the idea came when someone threw away their meat grinder, and I found it. They probably thought that because of the shortage they would never use it again.

I ran to the river, took my bath, stole some nice clothes, and went to work trying to find a buyer. It was easy. I told them that I was from the country and because we were so poor, I had butchered my prize cow to sell as hamburger. Everyone bought my story hook, line, and sinker. At night, I would catch the rats and grind my "hamburger." Then at dawn the following morning, I would sell it. Some of the people complained of the taste, but I told them that it was the hormones we fed my cow to help her win prizes.

I know some of you think that I was wrong in doing this, but it was only going to be for a little while, and, besides, people did get their meat. I only told a little white lie when I said that the meat came from my cow, isn't that the way to run a business?

I soon had all my friends working for me catching the rats and grinding them up, and my business grew. In one year I had enough money to go home and buy my parents' old house. Most importantly, I was able to help all of my friends, who now live with me.

We have a thriving business, but we don't sell rats anymore; we bake bread and sell it. That seemed right for Mother's old house. We have since moved into a bigger house, because we are always finding another homeless child to bring home.

I still have my questions of morality. I am always wondering if it is right to help those other kids or should I let them experience life for themselves, the way I did.

As for me, what I have learned is that people don't judge me so much as to how I got my money, but rather, they judge me on how I use it.

Another minor pretend game on this level is the one of detachment versus attachment. Initially the game is played like this: the people who are attached to things pretend that God can be found in material things, and the people who practice detachment pretend that God is not in those same physical things. They try to get rid of them to make room for God to come into their lives. The people who have things and "important" relationships with them try to prove to the rest of the world that they have God-like powers because they can bring all this stuff into their lives. On the other hand, the detached people pretend they have God-like powers because they can survive without material possessions.

As in all games, when we find contrasts, it generally means that we have a false premise. Obviously, the false premise exists because of an erroneous focus. The attachers are pretending they are not God, and as such. they are trying to transfer their God-hood to something outside themselves. As God, we are a part of everything in the universe. What possible difference could it make if we pretend we are either attached or detached from everything? Neither one has the capacity to make us God, since we already are. We can actually have as little or much as we want as long as we have the conscious awareness that we are God.

We can also see two types of relationships existing on this plane. On the one hand, we have those very pious people who refuse any type of relationship because it may distract them from their goal of finding God. Another person may have as many relationships as possible. Both have as their primary intent the gaining of acceptance from their peers to show that they have God-like capabilities.

The Ethical Ring generally requires a leader, teacher, or guru. This is someone who is pretending to have a close connection with God, and like all the other student-teacher games this Ring assumes that one person has more knowledge than the other. Usually in this game, though, the knowledge comes from doing the rituals for a longer amount of time.

One person who attained a level of mastery at the Ethical Ring level was Paramahansa Yogananda. He taught his disciples according to Sri Kriyananda, who was one of his disciples and the author of the book <u>The Path</u>, which teaches the concept of celibacy and that marriage is only a substitute for a relationship with God. To further play within this concept, he divided his ashrams into male and female sections and had a standing rule that if they were to ever meet a person of the opposite sex, they could not look into their eyes.

As moths come to the light, so it seems disciples come to a Master. These relationships appear to be part of the student-teacher games, but in reality they entail much more. A true master knows he or she has no new knowledge to offer disciples, because the Master knows the disciples are already God. The Master understands that they come to learn what the game is all about, so the Master devises activities that allow students to learn by making them experience the contrasts the game has to offer. To do this effectively, a Master must be clever.

Yogananda was correct in his statement (I am sure he would appreciate me telling him that) that often marriage is a substitute for a relationship with God. Man, in his attempt to pretend he is not God and that God is outside of himself, thinks God can more easily be found in someone or something else. Especially if we are playing within this Ring, we may marry as a way to find God. If we deem that a person is "higher" spiritually than we are, we might marry them hoping that they can pull us along the path with them, and sometimes they do. The game basically is: if you love me you will take me to God.

Yogananda probably suspected that his disciples had sexual experiences before they joined him, or at least it was a fair assumption. Therefore, he knew that they had experienced that part of the game. So the only way he could get them to experience the contrast was to incorporate celibacy into his discipline. This allowed the transfer of focus from sexual activity to non-sexual activity.

Many of the games within this level deal with what are now termed as "spiritual concepts." These concepts include celibacy, humility, detachment, trust, beliefs, and so on. As with all games, the proper environment must be established before the games can be played. Yogananda's ashram, as an example, provided a perfect environment for the initiates to experience celibacy as well as many of the other spiritual concepts. This environment had strict rules and allowed protection. Only after we experience these concepts in a safe environment can we then apply them to the worldly games. This is when the real fun begins.

These concepts are fairly easy to handle in a safe environment. But how do we handle the concept of celibacy when surrounded by sexually active people? Likewise, it is rather easy to be humble when the only jobs we get to do all day long are menial, i.e., housecleaning, digging ditches, etc. The real test of humility comes when we become the president of a major company.

It is fairly easy to be detached if we have achieved little, but how do we handle it when we own a mansion and a Porsche.

The safe environment concept has been around for a long time; even John the Baptist hid in a cave for many years. The problem with the creation of this type of environment is that it limits our experiences. It was an acceptable practice during the Piscean Age, but now that we are in the Aquarian Age, we need more opportunities for growth through relationships. In many ways, the Piscean Age created a focus on ritual and concept, whereas the New Age is more about experiences. As with all games, the evolutionary process requires that they become progressively more intense. We will now find that within a marriage situation we can test the limits of our religious concepts. For instance, we naturally have an arena to see what the contrasts are between being celibate and being sexually active. If we decide to test the limits of celibacy, how better to experience it than to climb into bed with your sexual partner every night? The game becomes greatly magnified; the limits we have set for the game become expanded.

In many ways, a marriage situation based on the precepts of this Ring, offers us a safe environment where we can maintain our rituals. Couples working at the Ethical Ring level must consciously explore the rituals they mutually establish for themselves and stay focused on the concepts they are exploring. One of the primary lessons available to learn within this Ring is that activity is just that, activity. There should be no judgment on our part nor should we see any activity as good or bad. We are just playing games and enjoying them as such. If we judge them we complicate the game, and in many cases, the judging process curtails our enjoyment. Granted, we may make a wrong choice from time to time, but it is not bad, just as making a right choice is not good. Making choices is a part of the game.

One key to enlightenment is to make choices that allow us to perform "right actions." Within each choice we make, we will find options that let us make a right choice for ourselves, for others, or that will do both. The choice that enables everyone involve to have their needs satisfied is probably the choice we could make.

Of the three Rings already discussed, this Ring seems to offer the most complicated concepts. It is very easy for initiates at this level to take their games very seriously. As with all games, when we take them seriously, our heaviness takes us to an endarkenment position. Enlightenment comes only by approaching the games lightly. For best results, rituals should always be fun. They are just games and should be approached that way. Have we ever seen a picture of a Master deep in meditation that did not include a smile on his face? Have we ever looked into a Master's eyes and not seen a twinkle? Masters become enlightened because they take the games lightly.

There is a fundamental need, a fundamental drive in all humans to always do the "right" thing from a moral perspective. This drive is fueled by an energy called "conscience." Our conscience will never let us perform an immoral act. It will not let us lie, cheat, steal, commit adultery, covet thy neighbor's ass (or any other part of them), or anything else it deems as immoral. So how do we get away with it? P. D. Ouspensky in his book In Search of the Miraculous tells us what his teacher Georges Gurdjieff has to say about it.

> *If a man whose entire world is composed of contradictions were suddenly to feel all these contradictions simultaneously within himself, if he were to feel all at once that he loves everything he hates and hates everything he loves; that he lies when he tells the truth and that he tells the truth when he lies; and if he could feel the shame and horror of it all, this would be the state which is called 'conscience'. A man cannot live in this state; he must either destroy contradictions or destroy conscience. He cannot destroy conscience, but if he cannot destroy it he can put it to sleep, that is, he can separate by impenetrable barriers one feeling of self from another, never see them together, never feel their incompatibility, the absurdity of one existing alongside the other.*
>
> *But fortunately for man, that is, for his peace and for his sleep, this state of consciousness is very rare. From early childhood 'buffers' begin to grow and strengthen him, taking from him the possibility of seeing his inner contradictions and therefore, for him, there is no danger whatever of a sudden awakening.(Ouspensky, 1949, p.156)*

So as we saw with our discussions on health, we can also close down the channels of our conscience and stop that natural God-like flow which takes us to a moral state of right action. It requires inner work to rid ourselves of these buffers. Even if we are stuffed with buffers, there is always at least one instant when we feel a twinge of guilt, and that is our clue that we need to do some inner work.

Guilt is not always a good diagnostic tool however, because it can come from many sources other than moral issues. Sometimes we can even feel guilty doing something we know is positively the right thing, but what guilt does show us is that something is wrong within our belief system.

So when we are able to notice this twinge of guilt, which in itself is difficult, we need to ask why it is there. Then we can evaluate our feelings and try to clear out the buffers that keep us from right action.

Allowing our conscience to rule our actions insures morally right actions, which relieves us of the burden of having to judge everything we or someone else does. Following our conscience takes us to a path of freedom by reducing the chaos in our lives.

Besides using the twinge of guilt as a guide, an even better guide is judgment. The act of judging someone else's actions is always based on our moral perspective, and is, therefore, always a way to encourage others to believe in our morality and our God-like qualities. Our conscience will never judge another, because it knows there is not a universal right and wrong.

There is a difference between morality and conscience: morality is the established right and wrong that comes from our environment, whereas conscience is the innate part of us that knows what is right or wrong for us. In a moral sense, we may feel that stealing is wrong, but our conscience innately knows that given the right circumstance, stealing may be the appropriate action. The previous little story illustrates such a case. Morally the girl felt that stealing was wrong, but her conscience saw no alternative. At one time, stealing was apparently the appropriate choice, later in her life it wasn't.

The buffer that Gurdjieff talks about is the sometimes monstrous chasm existing between morality and conscience. If the church, for example, says it is immoral to use birth control, but our conscience knows that we are not capable of raising a kid, then a chasm develops. If it remains unresolved, then we become candidates for the loony bin. Therefore, in order to avoid relinquishing ourselves to a state of psychosis, we must pretend that the moral decision of the church is right (and it is what we are going to follow forcing us to throw our conscience into some hidden cavern of our mind), or we must leave the church. There is a very good chance that everything we can list as having to do with morality can fall into this dualistic category.

Morality allows us to be law-abiding citizens or members of a certain sect, while conscience allows us to be who we are and follow the path of freedom. Morality, in a generalized sense (forgetting all the nuances that come from unique environments), is intended to make us all the same. Conscience makes us individual.

There are some moral codes which will be in line with our conscience, but they will be specific items and not comprise whole agendas. Therefore, in general, we basically need to throw away the things we think make up our morality because they are someone else's. Take one moral issue, find people with the same questions around the same issue, and explore the intricacies of it to see if it really resonates with our soul; this is the way of clearing out the garbage, the buffers, that prevent the surfacing of our conscience.

**We become enlightened on this level
when morality and conscience become as one.**

I would also like to mention the Alcoholic Anonymous concept of morality, since during this cycle in our history we have so many programs designed around its twelve steps. A.A. was set up on the premise that before someone would be willing to change their lifestyle (abstain from alcohol, drugs, or other addiction) and join their program, they would first have to "hit bottom." It was and is generally assumed that the bottom is physically related: they lose their job, family, or health. On the surface, this apparently happens, but hitting the bottom really goes much deeper. The bottom referred to in A.A. is really the bottom of the Ethical level referred to here. When this happens, morality no longer makes sense.

An alcoholic or addict goes through life performing what they perceive to be right actions, as we all do. But as their right actions become further and further from their conscience, the stress created from this friction eventually becomes unbearable. Their compensatory reaction initially becomes one of consuming more alcohol or drugs to avoid this stress, but when they sober up, their guilt is dramatic. It is the motivation to get rid of guilt that drives so many addicts to these meetings in order to the recover their true selves.

There are many geneticists and biochemists that say alcoholism is a genetically based disease caused by a chemical imbalance. Even A.A. calls it a disease, and they may be right, but so what? If a person didn't drink, there would be no way that he would exhibit alcoholic behavior. There is only one reason why a person drinks, takes drugs, or has another addiction and that is because they see it as a right action. For it to be a right action implies that it is an inherent part of their moral code. If morally it is a right action, then there is no therapy that can help a person quit. The only therapy that can possibly help is to first show them that they are drinking not because of some personal disease or social disease that is out of their control, but because there is some part of them that sees it as a right action. Then the person needs to evaluate why they believe it to be a right action, and at what point in their life did it become a part of their morality. Hopefully when the person sees that what they think is right action is only action based on a false perception, then that will no longer be a right action for them. In other words, if they grew up and saw their mother, father, brother, sister, aunt, or uncle drinking either socially or to drown their problems, then that action can only be deemed as an appropriate way of being in the world, a right action given the same circumstances. If the permission for the action did not come from family, then it could have come from peers, television, or the movies. There has to be some event in the alcoholic's life that told them that drinking was okay. It may even be as subtle as their parents taking them out to dinner and they saw apparently successful people drinking and enjoying themselves.

This can be translated into other areas of their life as well, since many will steal for drug money, be abusive, lie, cheat, etc. There has to be some instance in their life that gave them the morality that made it a right action to do those things.

Step Four of the Twelve Step Program covers this somewhat, as it requires the participant to make a moral inventory of themselves. This step more than any other requires the help of another, generally their sponsor, to educate them as to what is right action. This is extremely difficult since true right actions are individual, but the sponsor (if nothing else is accomplished), can show that the participant's interpretation of moral action is different from their true right action.

It does no good to discuss right action from an intellectual viewpoint, because it can not be incorporated into a person's morality through an analytical approach; it requires an emotional acceptance.

To use an example, if we get a normal, everyday-type of camera, we can take a two dimensional picture and we say to ourselves "Isn't that pretty?" (an analytical evaluation of the picture). However, if we took the same picture with laser photography we would have a three-dimensional picture that would look real. To take a laser picture requires that two different light rays merge together, not just the one with normal photography. Karl Pribraum has a theory that we store memories in our mind like a hologram (laser photography), which would include our morality. So if that is true, we store our morality by first recognizing a concept (one ray of energy) and then reinforce it with some sort of emotion (the second ray of energy), thereby giving us our holographic memory of what we now perceive as right action. From this we can see how either an analytical or an emotional approach by themselves will not initiate change; it needs to be a combination.

So when someone stands up at an A.A. or similar meeting and tells everyone a memory they experienced as a drunk/addict either logically or emotionally i.e., "I was facing death every day" or something similar, this reinforces the old behavior. However, when someone tells of a new "right action" they discovered and the group gets excited and identifies with it, then there is a chance that a new right action can be incorporated.

There was a program I heard of that was trying to treat the addict/alcoholic on an outpatient basis. From what I heard from the participants, every session was spent focused on the members of the group who had relapsed the day before. The leader of the group had the relapser tell the group about why and how they relapsed. From what I heard, all this program did was to reinforce the old patterns. The one girl I knew who went through this program lost her two months of sobriety and, in addition, met new drug dealers and learned new ways to scam. The group leader obviously thought that an analytical approach and mild confrontation would solve the problem, but in essence, all he did was reinforce their old patterns.

The key to any therapy has to revolve around the concept of right action. If the patient is feeling any amount of guilt, then the question of morality must be raised. The therapy revolves around right action as dictated by the patient's conscience, followed by supportive therapies to enhance those natural ethics.

Right actions are a touchy issue for most people, since almost everyone believes that their way is the only viable one. It is these people who create wars, and it is the Ethical Ring which fuels most if not all of them. To have a war, one group of people must believe that their way is right and that their opponents are performing wrongful acts: a truth for both sides. Whether it be the Crusades of the Middle Ages, the American Revolution, civil wars, or Vietnam, both sides knew without a doubt that their actions were the right actions, and a drive to resolve differences caused both parties to push their morality on the other at any cost.

There may be some that wish to disagree with me by saying "No, it was not morality, but greed." Greed is a byproduct of morality. The holding onto and accumulation of money is a morality-driven right action to some.

In conclusion, we are faced with two different sets of rules in which to play our games. One is the innate set that tells us what our right action should be in any given situation. This is driven by conscience. If we lived by this set of ethics, we would find the world a different place, because everyone would be a true individual and we would not want anything from each other. Actions derived from our conscience are pure and take us along our path without detour.

The other set of rules we play by comes to us from outside ourselves. This set is termed our "morality." Morality instructs us to perform certain actions for the benefit of others in order to make us more socially acceptable. Morality strips us of our individuality and turns us into robots; it leads us into group activities, gives us prejudices, and takes us into endarkenment.

With the understanding of this level, our quantum leap toward enlightenment is fantastic because no longer do we need to criticize or look down on others, for we know that everyone is always performing what they think are right actions. We will also understand that other's actions aren't conscience driven. We will understand that no matter what is said or done, their perception of right action will remain until they hit their bottom. Then, and only then, is there a chance for change.

To become a part of the solution requires that we move toward conscience motivation. When we are performing true right actions, it creates a greater friction within the "Universal Unconscious," which in turn causes more people to hit the bottom and start asking for help.

Because the concept of right action is so confusing, I would like to end this chapter with a story called:

## The Myth of Power

Once in a far and distant land lived a very gracious king. He would give whatever he had to anyone in need. The people of his land prospered and grew; they were very happy and lived carefree lives.

One day the town crier walked through the land yelling, "Beware of impending doom!" He had a feeling that things were too good and according to what he could glean from history, he knew that eventually it had to end.

The people jeered and made fun of him, thinking that surely the town crier had gone off the deep end and was completely crazy. But the more they ridiculed him, the louder the crier shouted his words of doom, making him even more convinced that he was right in his analysis of the situation.

Word of his actions spread throughout the kingdom until it had reached the King. The King sat in utter amazement when he was told what the crier had said. The King's mouth dropped and tears welled up in this eyes. He left his throne and retired to his chambers, where he sulked for fourteen days.

At the end of his mourning period, he returned to his throne and summoned all of his Chiefs of Staff. He brought in the Secretary of State, the Secretary of Defense, the Secretary of Health, Education and Welfare, the Secretary of the Interior, and his Secretary of Astrology. He sat staring at each one of them as they entered the great hall, one by one, until they all had entered. Then he spoke, "Where have I gone wrong?" he asked. "I have tried to make this a kinder, gentler nation. I reduced inflation, increased the GNP, and have created a state of peace and well being. Yet, one person dares to predict the end of all of this. How can we prevent even the remotest possibility of this happening?"

The Secretary of State spoke first. He said, "Our intelligence sources think that this man may have been brainwashed by our neighboring country to the North. This country is very jealous of how happy we are, and they would love to see us collapse into a pile of ashes. It is our learned opinion that they are behind this and that a covert plan should be developed to undermine their King and reduce them to a pile of ashes before they do it to us." The Secretary of State smiled, flicked the ashes off his big cigar onto the floor, and sat back in his seat, pleased with his assessment of the situation. The King was shocked. He had no idea that he had enemies. He thought the King to the North was his friend.

The King then looked at the Secretary of Defense and asked his opinion. "Well," the fat old gentleman blurted in his raspy, very deep voice, "to be honest, we have not seen much military action to the North. We have, however, taken aerial photographs of the land in the South, and have seen activity that could be a build-up of arms." The fat cat sat back and continued, "If you remember, the Secretary of State asked you a year ago for some money to give to these dangerous people in the South. We feel that the money was used to build up their military, not for schools as they promised. Our aerial photographs show many new buildings being erected, and we can only assume they have some military significance. We, too, believe that this town crier is a spy, and he is trying to create fear among our people, making it much easier for invaders to come through our land and demolish us."

The King raised his eyebrows at this statement, for he loved the King of the South as he would his own brother. They had previously chatted endlessly into the night and had agreed on many concepts. Of all the surrounding Kings, the King of the South was his favorite.

It was now the Secretary of Health's turn. "Your Majesty," he said, "I think this relates to the problem I have been telling you about. It is obvious that we need more mental health facilities in our country. From what I hear from the peasants, the problem is simply that this man is crazy. If we could put several billion more dollars into my budget, we could prevent lunatics like the town crier from roaming the land and creating havoc.

If you look at the record, you will see that you keep funneling more and more money to our neighboring countries and, at the same time, more and more to our defense. If we didn't send so much money to other the countries, those countries wouldn't have the money to build their armies, and we wouldn't have to build such a massive defense system. That is an understandable circle, but there is only so much money and something has to suffer. What has suffered is the health, education, and welfare of our people. The town crier represents an omen of things to come because of our deteriorating condition. Our statistical studies show that soon we will see thousands like him, maybe even worse off. We may someday even find our parks and streets full of these mentally ill people."

"Oh, my God!" The King exclaimed, as he grabbed his chest and rocked back in this throne propelling his crown across the floor. Once the King regained his composure and the Secretary of Defense had captured his crown and graciously returned it, the King bellowed, "No, no, that's impossible. Our society represents the cream of the crop in the world. We are the most prosperous country in the world. No, no, it could never happen here, could it?"

He threw the question with his eyes to the Secretary of the Interior. Of the all the King's men, the Secretary of the Interior was the simplest. He was raised in the country and loved his position, since he spent most of his time in the country's parks. He took a deep breath and sighed. "Gosh, I don't know. I've never thought about it. I do know if I was homeless, I would love to go live in a park." He widened his eyes as if he had come upon a great idea or finally understood what was happening. He looked the King straight in the eyes and continued at a more excited pace, "If it is possible that our people would come and live in our parks, then we ought to plan for that as a contingency. After all, wouldn't we rather have them live in a park than on the streets?

Yes, yes, I'm sure that the answer to this dilemma is to increase the Department of Interior's budget so that we can buy more land, do some major construction, and get things ready, just in case. In fact, we ought to install bomb shelters in our parks just in case we do get attacked as the Secretaries of Defense and State have suggested. I even know of a company who could do a great job, my brother has built lots of them overseas. Yes, yes I am sure this is the proper answer to the problem.

Because this program will be so expensive, I would also suggest that we sell the mineral rights we have on several of our big tracts. If you give me the go ahead, I could raise enough money to pay for this whole thing. Besides mineral rights, we have acres of timber that could be sold. We would need to relocate some Indian reservations, but that wouldn't be any problem. Just give them a little Red Eye, and we can get what we want from them. Yes, yes it would work. I can solve everything for you, if you'll just give me the go ahead."

The King was looking straight at him with his head tilted to the side. He had a look of puzzlement on his face. The King felt he was face-to-face with another mad man. Not only did he have a mad town crier on his hands, he had a latent psychotic in his group of advisors.

The King dropped his head and rubbed his forehead. He was exhausted and felt a headache coming on. He was more confused now than before he started.

The only advisor left that could possibly offer some insight to the King was the Secretary of Astrology. He was a man of few words, but when he spoke, everyone listened. He was much more than an astrologer, and many wondered if he used astrology at all, or if it was just a front for his mysticism.

He did dress the part; he wore a long robe with brightly colored astrological symbols covering its surface. His hair was long and unkempt and flowed graciously into his long, graying beard, None of his fellow advisors liked him because he had thwarted their efforts to attain increased power on many occasions. He definitely was not one of the boys. He could quiet the group with a stare.

The King enjoyed having his Astrologer close to him. He had the feeling that much of his power came from the old astrologer. Yet, he knew on some level he drove the old wizard nuts with his silly little questions.

Who was the old guy? Was he a friend, a father, a brother, or a teacher to the King. No one knew for sure, including the King, for he was all of them. Rumor had it that he used to have his own Kingdom and gave it up to work towards some personal goals. Being a king took too much of his time and entailed too many problems that needed his constant attention. He had realized that if he wanted to grow personally and spiritually, he needed more freedom, so he denounced his throne and sought the quietude of the forest. It was there in the forest that he studied, transformed his life, and met the future King.

The King cleared his throat, bringing the wizard out of his constant semi-trance, dreamy state. The wizard looked at the King and saw confusion and fear in his eyes. It reminded him of the first time he met the little King boy. The wizard did not talk, he just stared back at the King.

"Well, my old friend," the King blurted out disrupting the quiet hall, "what is your assessment of what is happening and what has been said here today?"

The wizard sat in silence, stroking his beard. Finally after what seemed an eternity he said, "My assessment, if you will permit me to make one, is that everyone is correct in their evaluation to some degree.

Firstly, the country to the North is a very powerful beast and although it would like to see us reduced to rubble, it stands still because it has no head.

Secondly, the country to the South is somewhat the opposite. It has a head, but it has an emaciated body. The head eats well, but never swallows, depriving its body of basic nutrients.

Thirdly, the mental well-being of our land is depressed because although your subjects appear to be happy, they do not grow. Where all needs are met, ingenuity dies.

And fourthly, the parks of this nation are important as a way for man to return to nature. The Indians do not need to be relocated, but rather they should be given the job of protecting the parks.

So that is my rebuttal to the opinions expressed today at this meeting. That is all except for one, yours, my gracious King. You asked if you have gone wrong in your management of your kingdom, and whether one man's opinion is necessarily an omen of things to come. You have asked us all to evaluate what is right and what is wrong, but we can not answer a question of morality pertaining to your personal perceptions. Is there really such a concept as wrong actions or, for that matter, right actions? Can a wrong decision lead to the doom of a nation if it is not time for that nation to dissolve into the ethers of history?

All of your actions to date have been both right and wrong and, at the same time, neither right or wrong. You see, my friend, you can only direct a course of action, you can not judge it. So the answer to the question of what you have done wrong is an answer that only you can discover."

The King nodded as if he understood. Then he stood, left the massive hall, and went to the woods he so loved as a boy.

***

*Therefore the sage takes care of all men*
*and abandons no one.*
*He takes care of all things*
*and abandons nothing.*
        *—The Tao*

# Chapter 8

## Conscious Ring (Fourth Heaven)

The Conscious Ring is the last level which helps us define who we are and the nature of our psyche. It is the Ring that identifies our "I," and we do it by examining our feelings around our actions on the Physical, Mental, and Ethical Ring levels.

Our feelings or how we perceive ourselves in relation to either our activities or other people gives us the fourth variable in our chaos formula. Understanding that our feelings are just another variable simplifies the chaos, although for the non-conscious initiate, it may seem inseparable from the previous Rings. Our feelings are a great gift, because they can either completely cloud our actions or help us clarify them.

The "electron ring" of this Ring circles through the Root Chakra and the Crown Chakra. This represents the highest and the lowest experiences of man. It can allow us to soar into the skies or penetrate deep into the earth. We can experience contrasts of maximum love versus maximum fear, maximum lightness versus maximum heaviness, and awareness versus blindness.

We can see more distinctly within this Ring the differences of our mental outlooks as we alter our focus. Simply by moving our eyes we can change our feelings. If we consciously look down, we can experience extreme heaviness. If we consciously look up, we can experience lightness and optimism. We can learn that although our activities remain the same, by just changing our focus we can be happy or sad, optimistic or pessimistic, heavy or light.

As a result, the Conscious-initiate can experience more power and freedom than in any of the previous Rings. We learn to not only control our own actions, but find it easy to have power over others, as well. With a clear mind, we also find it easy to read the thoughts of others and play the game called "clairvoyance," which allows us to see the future and past.

The games of Conscious Ring are intended to bring the initiate to a new state of consciousness that has been described as an "awakened state." Of course, to pretend to be awakened means that first we must have pretended to be asleep. Within this Ring we seek to understand our position relative to the whole of things. We do this by observing how and why we react to different stimuli.

Psychology is the study of this interplay between "I" and the experience. For the most part, it deals with perception—as the way in which we view the world. Primarily, psychology tries to apply our perception of earlier games to explain why we are playing our current games the way we are. In other words, as a child, if we had a certain event happen to us, there is a good chance that how we perceived it will influence all future games. For instance, if our father hit us when we were a baby, then we may create as a reality that men are mean, or love is expressed by hitting, or any number of things depending on how we saw the rules to the game unfold.

Psychology has developed many protocols to help us discover our initial truths and understand that for the most part they are not really truths at all, but strictly perceptions of truth. Our search for truth is another way to allow us to search for God. We can create and find as many truths as we want. But there is only one truth and it is that we are God. Every other truth that is uncovered lets us pretend that God is hidden and must be identified.

Psychology can be divided into three groups each relating to a specific Ring: behavioral (physical), psychoanalysis (mental) and humanistic (ethical). Behavioral psychology, instead of looking directly at perceptions, deals with how we respond to the games we are playing and teaches us how to play better. Whereas, psychoanalysis looks at why we establish and define our game rules. And finally, humanistic psychology, the newest of them all, looks at our disciplines and rituals and how we feel about them.

The Conscious-initiate uses all forms of psychology. First, we constantly work on simplifying the rules in all the games we are playing by trying to separate the illusory truths from the real truth. Second, we try to learn to enjoy all those games.

Behavioral psychology was developed by B.F. Skinner and deals primarily with a person's actions in relation to their environment. Briefly, Skinner breaks behavior into two categories: respondent behavior which refers to a specific behavior invoked by a specific stimulus and operant behavior which defines actions we perform in order to manipulate our environment. He also believes that a behavior can not become a way of being unless it is reinforced. This is the basis for aversion therapy, where the established rewards are drastically changed giving a negative reinforcement or punishment from the norm. This describes many of our actions of the Survival Ring, but how do we use this knowledge to find freedom from our behaviors?

Behaviorists have found that the "normal" behavior of a person, as he plays his games, moves between loving to play and hating to play. If we were to express this range mathematically, it would be shown as a wave with all its ups and downs. This tells us that as we play our games, we respond to them in a cyclic manner: love them, then hate them, then love them, etc.

The initiate understands this and therefore seems to ride the waves easier and does not get upset when on the downward side. We try to enjoy the highs as well as the lows and learn that our behavior is cyclic with regard to everything in our universe, including our activities, our relationships, our spiritual growth, and our learning ability.

In this way, we learn to identify the cycle and try to further enhance both its highs and lows, trying to go higher on the high cycle and lower on the low cycle, knowing that it is just our perception of the game that shifts the cycle. By riding and accepting this cycle, we can uncover the truths of why and how we participate in this particular game, and why our behavior is the way it is.

As we observe the cycles, we learn how multifaceted we really are, in that we play many games during the course of a day. We also find there are some games we truly love to play and others we don't. Or even within a game, there may be certain facets of the game we enjoy and others we don't. The cycles in our life help us to identify and define who our "I" really is by showing us the contrasts between our likes and dislikes.

Within the established behavioral wave theory, we experience the upper apex of the wave when we do things we like doing and the lower apex when we do things we don't.

After watching ourselves play within these cycles of life, we notice that we experience different feelings depending on which apex we are participating in at any given time. When we are at one of the lower apexes, our focus will primarily be on the heavier aspects of life—we experience fear, worry, doubt, unfulfilled expectations, or even that we are not loved. In many respects, we feel a maximum feeling of separation from God.

While on the upper apex, we experience feelings of the opposite scope— we feel light, happy, everything in the world is running smooth, even a certain amount of control over our life and, in essence, we are attuned to our Godhood.

We find several different teachings on how to deal with the cycle concept when we research esoteric teachings. The most commonly accepted way is through the use of discipline. Discipline is the act of forcing ourselves from the lower apex to the higher. If we have discipline then we force ourselves to go through unpleasant tasks. Hopefully, if we force ourselves enough times we will learn to enjoy those tasks. Discipline appears to represent a contradiction in terms: being unhappy in order to make ourselves happy, but it is valid because happiness is just a point of view. In many cases, by forcing ourselves to do a dismal project shows us that it is not so bad. With enough of these projects, we may find that we can do anything and find joy. Usually, to interest a prospective student in participating in a discipline requires that a reward must be promised: a promised enlightenment maybe?

The second way is to only do the things we like doing. As we proceed through our daily games, we try to choose which ones to play and which ones not to. This process can work also, but it is very difficult without a lot of self-control and a good teacher to help us. The games come at us so fast sometimes, we usually find it is very hard to be discreet. Then, all of a sudden, we find ourselves involved in a game we didn't want to play.

For example, several years ago I developed a process whereby people could find a satisfying career. I called it the "Ultimate Path Principle." This process is started by having the interested person list all of the business skills he or she has already learned. Then add to the list his or her hobbies or interests that possibly could be turned into a career, even if he or she doesn't currently know how it might be possible. Then he or she reviews the list and checks off all the activities listed that he or she thoroughly enjoys doing. In this way, the list can be whittled down to the person's five favorite things. Those five items are then combined together to indicate a possible new career. His or her career would then include five of his or her favorite things. All of the hundreds of people that have gone through this process were pleased with the possibilities, but only a handful had the courage to follow this guidance, and they all are very happy now with their new careers. The key to the Ultimate Path Principle is that it gives us a plan using the things that we enjoy to take us to the upper apex—a major bliss!

The third approach to these cycles is to just ride the wave and learn to enjoy the roller coaster ride. The initiate using this technique is primarily learning how all the aspects of a cycle are important in finding our "I." Often, we will create lower apex situations just because we feel we can learn more about ourselves through opposition. How much can a person really learn if everything is perfect? Our focus is primarily on the lower apexes, and we feel if we can learn to love our feelings and actions there, that by the very nature of the definition, the lower apexes will become non-existent. This approach represents the opposite of the second approach.

The main problem with this concept is that sometimes the initiate loves the feelings of struggle, fear, worry, and heaviness so much, that they create a life where this is the "norm" and they never get to experience the contrast of the upper apexes. This example is similar to that of those poor people who learn to love their misery and life of self-sacrifice.

Our goal in watching our cycles is not to remain at either the top or the bottom, but to rest in the middle. We need to attain a level of balance, which means eliminating the highs and the lows in our lives.

These, of course, are all games. Just as the electron rings do not really exist, the wave really doesn't exist either. We pretend that things are cyclic so we have an excuse to pretend we have emotions and feelings. Pretending that there really is a behavioral cycle adds another dimension to our games. So now we have the activity involved in the game as well as the knowledge of the game. We also have the moral aspects, how and why we are playing, and mood changes. Isn't this fun? These things are just analogies and do not represent a hidden truth.

Again, the major pretend game is that we are separate from God and therefore separate from the whole. The games we play are intended to prove to ourselves that we are in fact individuals—that we exist totally on our own; while, at the same time, we have the goal of becoming one with everything.

In this Ring we pit the power of the conscious mind against the power of the subconscious mind, as we try to identify our true identity. The psychology that discusses this theory was developed by Sigmund Freud and is called psychoanalysis. Because we are exploring the components of our mind, we can see how this falls in line with Mental Ring. Also, we find that the therapists who work with Freud's concepts are themselves entrenched in the concept of reasoning, and, therefore, every action performed must have a reason behind it. Freud believed that our perception of one's environment, especially as related to the five growth stages (oral, anal, phallic, latency, and genital), makes up our personality and how we function in the world. According to this psychology, only by uncovering these perceptions can we discover who we really are. Everything we do has an explanation, a reason.

Freud perceived a tremendous chasm between a person's conscious mind and what he termed the "unconscious mind." He felt it analogous to an iceberg with the visible tip the conscious and the hidden massive part (which is seen) the unconscious. The methodology used to communicate with the unconscious are called "Freudian slips" and dream therapy; both are exercises in analytics. His therapeutic goal was to reduce the gap between what the conscious mind perceived as truth and what the unconscious knew was truth.

As a Conscious-initiate we use Freud's precepts when we perform self-analysis. We represent our consciousness to be ourselves, and our subconsciousness (unconscious according to Freud) to be God. Science tells us that we only use ten percent of our brain, implying to the Conscious Ring initiate that God remains ten times bigger and more powerful than we are. Because of this, we spend most of our time trying to open up our subconscious mind. To do this, we primarily use the disciplines of concentration, meditation, and contemplation.

The first step in all activities of this Ring, is to learn to turn our thought processes on and off. We have learned since early childhood how to turn our thoughts on, but very few people have ever learned to turn them off. The game of concentration teaches us how to turn our thoughts off. By focusing very hard on something and concentrating, we soon learn that we can shut off the chatter that is constantly running through our minds. This shows us the mental contrast of thought versus non-thought.

Once we learn to shut off this "thought chatter," we will learn the power of silence. We learn that much more can be learned from silence than from "thought noise."

The other great advantage of silence is that it is a great energy saver. Our normal thought process takes energy to operate, but without these constant thoughts, we can store most of that energy. As people who play the poor financial game must give their money away, so we find that those that play the tired game must give away all their energy. We lose this energy by either constantly talking or thinking; for many people it seems rather difficult to do both at the same time.

Probably one of the simplest exercises to develop the power of concentration was presented by Ram Das. He instructs his students to concentrate on their breathing and count each breath, with the condition that if they catch their mind wandering, they must start all over again. The object of this game is to reach five hundred, uninterrupted. He tells us that the achievement of this goal does not necessarily guarantee enlightenment, but it puts the student well on the path toward enlightenment. Without concentration and focus, nothing else is possible for the initiate.

Once the initiate has mastered the game of concentration, he is then able to proceed to the next step called "meditation." Currently, many teachers are teaching varied mental exercises and classifying them as meditation. These exercises range in scope from relaxation to visualization. Real meditation requires the mastery of concentration first. Without concentration techniques in hand, these exercises represent only the fun, mental activities of the Survival Ring or Mental Rings.

Within the framework of silence, meditation allows the initiate to bring into his mind one question at a time. Having only one thing in his mind allows full concentration on that question. In silence, he can view the question from every possible angle until he completely understands all the variables associated with it.

This is a different type of meditation than exists on the Ethical Ring level. The meditations of the Ethical-initiate allow silence, and within that silence we try to find God. However, without silence and focus, we find our prayers are seemingly empty.

As a Conscious-initiate, we know that our subconscious is a part of us, so when we seek answers to our questions, we see our meditation as a way to open up our memory. To add to the game, we may allow answers to come in the forms of analogies, metaphors, or visions. The meditative experience shows us new horizons not before conceived and gives us flashes of a "new consciousness."

The next step, contemplation, allows the initiate to enter into a question, a landscape, a sound, or an activity without any thinking process whatsoever. We enter with our mind in total silence. This allows us to totally experience without any expectations, judgment, or rationalization. We strive to experience whatever it is that we are focused on as just an experience, nothing more.

Our thoughts have a way of buffering our experiences. For instance, if we look at a sunset and say to ourselves, "This is beautiful," we must first compare it to all of the other sunsets we have seen. However, if we just look at it with no thoughts, we are able to receive a great experience. We generally use our thoughts to protect us from our experiences. Not so much from a safety standpoint, but more for protection of our ego. We often have a fear of allowing ourselves to just totally experience. Our ego rises up and realizes it could lose it's identity in the process of experience without mental control.

The initiate who has learned the art of deep contemplation, lays his soul open to the universe, and communes with the deepest mysteries of life and of God.

The third branch of psychology we use was developed by Carl Rogers and is called "humanistic psychology." Many of the newer psychological approaches are derivatives of Rogers' work and represent vitalistic approaches to the discovery of our "I." Rogers believes that every human is constantly "growing" in every endeavor as they strive for "actualization," the state of being fulfilled in every aspect of our life.

Whereas, Skinner looks at individual actions, and Freud looks for singular repressed or inhibited drives, Rogers looks at us as whole beings capable of making right decisions. He also sees that problems encountered along the way are there for the experience and, most importantly, we chose that path.

What humanistic psychology teaches us is that we are not robots, as Skinner implies, and that we aren't broken, as Freud says. We are individuals that have some importance on this earth plane, something to give to all humans, and we have a right to be here.

In summary, because the initiate is exploring who he is, the major contrast is usually between his self-importance and his non-importance. As we explore our conscious mind, we learn that it, in itself, is fairly non-consequential compared to the power we imagine is held within the subconscious mind. Self-importance leaves in the face of a greater power. We learn that our conscious mind can only control how we see and play the games. It becomes apparent to us that the games are controlled by the power of our subconscious mind and we really have no control in its operation. We also find that when we consciously try to set up our own games, that somehow they never turn out the way we expected. Eventually we will make a conscious decision to play the games as they were established by the greater power.

It is interesting to note how much energy and time we spend trying to control our experiences or meet expectations in order to establish our self-importance. In reality, the effort put forth in order to feel worthy usually ends up giving us the opposite result. We strive for that feeling of self-importance, which always remains an unfilled expectation, because there is always a greater power to reckon with.

When we believe we are all Gods, then there is no level of importance to achieve; we see every one as equal in all respects. There is no one more or less powerful than we are. When this knowledge is accepted, the games we are playing to establish our importance have to become either nonexistent or recognized for what they are, games. It is easy to see how Masters who understand this principle can become so humble. It should be clarified that humbleness does not imply that these Masters don't play games, it just means that they know they are no more important than anyone else.

# Chapter 9

## Precision Ring (Fifth Heaven)

As established so far in our model, all of our electron rings and all of our Rings have been housed within the physical aspects of ourselves: our body, brain, conscience, or unconscious (also known as the subconscious). There are varied aspects to our growth process, and how we interpret life is seemingly beyond the concepts we use to identify ourselves. The next three Rings in our model relate to these concepts and as would be expected, they are found outside the body. Whereas, the four previous Rings relate to specific actions (as previously discussed), the next three Rings are more general, more all-encompassing and offer us a process to move toward freedom. These are all concepts that can change our focus and create new avenues to interpret the actions of the first four Rings. Although classical Chakra Theory claims that there are Chakras beyond the physical body, we will leave the Chakras at this point in our model because they are less understandable here than in the first four Rings.

These next Rings only become important when we wish to move into the mastery realms of a particular Ring. These levels help achieve a level of proficiency, or as I like to say, a sense of master-hood, a freedom.

The Precision Ring is a tough Ring to get a handle on because it is so conceptual, but it is one we have already experienced hundreds of times in our lives. Precision Ring is the process of performing the right action at the right time, which brings to light the importance of understanding the Ethical Ring, for if we don't know the right action then right timing is irrelevant.

I know from my experience that I have hundreds, if not thousands, of incidents in my life that I wish I could relive so I could perform the right action at the right time. In my imagination, I see how the course of my life would have changed if I had acted differently at any given time. It is fascinating to imagine what I would be doing now if I had made that different action. Of course, from a deterministic reference, I did make the right action at the right time because I am where I am supposed to be.

On the other hand, I have had very strong intuitive impulses to do certain actions that I knew were perfect and they flopped. I used to say in describing these events, "I gave a party and no one came." Then, several years later, I might see someone copy my project and they would be amazingly successful. Gosh, it is hard to count how many times this has happened to me. I know I am not alone, because we can pull out the Federal Patent records and see many fantastic ideas that hit the market at the wrong time. So, right action can be learned, but right timing requires finesse.

The primary ingredient to right timing is patience—waiting until the game unfolds before making our move. We might make some minor moves initially to test the capabilities of our opponents or to "test the water," as the cliché goes, but we must wait for the proper time to make our key moves. Right timing cannot be forced.

As an analogy, if we went out to hunt a deer, the proper process is to pick a spot where a deer will most likely come strolling along, hopefully daydreaming. We pick the spot by understanding the principles behind the game (right action). Once the spot is located, the Master hunter will sit and wait for the deer to come (patience). When he finally sees the deer coming, he does not instantaneously try to shoot it, he waits for the right time and at that time performs the right action, (which will net him a beautiful photograph).

Only by luck does a non-Master perform these together. They may have the timing down correctly, but then they often mess up the action. Since we are all Masters, we know this. However, there are people who have a fear of success, so they may try shooting the deer while he is still a mile away, or they will scare the deer away and make their task more complicated. Likewise, we find people with a fear of failure who are afraid to shoot because they might miss. They represent the same concept but from a different prospective. Both are afraid to do the right action at the right time. Because the Master knows it is a game, he or she waits for the proper time to take his or her action and has enough self-confidence to know his or her action will be right.

In mythology, there are many stories of sorcerers who wait for an omen to show them either the right action, the right time, or both. To take it out of the mythical realm, we receive those omens constantly. By watching the games unfold, we are told which action we should take. Right timing is usually also easy to detect, because at the proper time it seems that the other players focus on us, usually with an unnatural pause. It is like they turn to us and say, "It's your turn." If we are not prepared with an action at that moment, the game will continue without us. What would happen to the deer hunter if when the deer was right next to him, he had to run back to camp to get his camera? The Master has to be prepared.

This reminds me of another story that goes like this:

## The Farm

Josh was at a point in his life when he was enjoying the rewards of all his business endeavors. Josh had everything he could possibly want from a materialistic standpoint: a good family, a great dog, and vacations to far away and exciting places. His life was perfect except for one thing, he hated his job. He was good at it, and showing people how to clean a toilet was financially rewarding, but it was not very stimulating.

One day, he was sitting in a coffee shop between appointments drinking his dark, black coffee and smoking his cigarettes when he smelled this strange, obnoxious odor. He sniffed around and realized it was himself; He was saturated with the smell of his toilet bowl cleaner. That was it. Josh knew it was time to get out of this business But what would he do?

Josh shrugged his shoulders in desperation because he thought cleaning toilets was all he could do. Then he reached across the table and grabbed the morning newspaper. By a stroke of luck, the paper fell open to an ad that said, "Farm for Sale." That was it. Anybody could be a farmer. All a person has to do is plant a seed, water it, harvest it, and then sell it. Yes, that ad might change his life.

He jumped up and ran out of the restaurant, but then he came back in to pay his bill. He drove home as fast as he could and announced to his family what his new plan was. They were a little skeptical, but after a lot of fast talking, he was able to convince them.

Josh emptied out his savings, turned in his resignation, and bought that farm. They moved into their new home amidst all the construction. The farm house was rather old and run-down and needed a lot of work. His wife was up to the task, though, and orchestrated the makeover like she had done it before. Josh had the feeling she was trying to turn it into a "city house," but that was O.K.; she was happy with her project.

While she was doing that, Josh took off to town to buy seeds. This was going to be fun. He knew from a marketing standpoint that to be competitive he needed to plant a crop unique to the area. Because everyone else was planting potatoes and corn, he decided to plant rice. He had to wait several weeks for his order to get shipped to the store, but he was excited when he picked it up, even with all the heckling he received from his fellow farmers.

Well, he planted that rice, watered it, and waited. This was a perfect life. He waited that whole summer and nothing grew but the weeds. Josh realized that he had outsmarted himself, and now he was in trouble: almost broke, no crop to sell, and bills due all over town. Even his family was starting to laugh at him. Big joke.

He became very humble that winter and started to listen and ask questions of the other farmers. They were all more than happy to tell him why he couldn't grow rice in this valley and why they grew what they did.

It seemed like it took years for spring to roll around, but it finally did. This time he did exactly what he was told down to the letter, and that included planting potatoes under a new moon.

Within a couple of weeks, Josh saw little green things peeking up from under the ground. He was so excited he ran over and yanked one of them out of the ground and ran as fast as his fat little legs would carry him to show his wife so she would understand, too, that everything was going to be all right. They danced and laughed and sang long into the night.

A week went by with him watching his crop from dawn till dusk with not much happening. This was driving him nuts; he was out of money and he needed to know what was happening. He walked into the center of his potato patch because he figured that's where the plants would be the hardiest and pulled one up to see how many potatoes he had. There weren't any. Maybe it was too early. So he tried this every day throughout the next week with like results.

Dejected, Josh went to town to see if he could find some answers to his problem. When he told his newly acquired farmer-friends what he had done they looked at him and started to laugh. In unison they said, " You pulled them up?" And with that they roared. They were laughing so hard they had tears running down their cheeks and were literally rolling on the ground. Josh was puzzled, what was so funny?

When they were finished, one of them said, "What was so funny was that we all have done the same thing! People think farming is easy: you plant a seed, water it, harvest it, and sell it. But all of that is the easy part, the hard part is being patient."

❦

To someone unaware of the Precision Ring, one might say we are superstitious because we have learned to wait for an omen to show us the right time to take our action. When an omen turns into a superstition, it becomes invalid. People follow superstitions due to ignorance. They choose to be superstitious because they are looking for easy access to this Ring.

What we are really talking about is a sense of awareness. To be a Master in a game requires one to become aware of everything that is happening. We learn to be aware of everyone's moves and counter moves, the object of the game from all of the players' perspectives, the playing field, and the other players. This awareness requires both concentration and focus. If we do not maintain a level of focus, we will know neither the right action nor the right time in which to make our move.

The Precision Ring initiate does not play the games for success or failure, for we know those are just perceptions. We play them to add a certain intensity to them. By playing the games properly, we experience more fun and joy in everything we do. The Master is usually the controlling factor in most games because he is the only one who is aware of all occurring events. Right action sometimes means to change the course of a game, and, sometimes, altering the course of a game can bring a smile to the face of the most casual observer.

As we enter into Precision Ring, we start to really understand the concept that this is truly a recreational planet. As we look at the other people around us, we see they are all involved in their own specific agendas. The ones who take their games the most seriously are usually the most fun to watch. We move into this Ring when we understand that the game we are playing is just a game.

Once we realize that we are playing a game, we might choose to experiment by taking our game into one of the other Rings by changing our focus and thereby the object of the game. The initiate has basically two choices: either we can keep the same object, but change the rules to conform to the new Ring or move into another game within the same Ring. Either is a proper step, but the former is usually more productive.

For instance, if we had a job and learned to play the "earning a living" game of the Survival Ring, our next step might be to move it to the Mental Ring level. We would then try to analyze why were able to perform so well at earning a living. In fact, we see this in business, where a person who makes a lot of money one year tries to establish an analytical system explaining why he did so well, and then the next year he or she is broke or writes a book. Maybe one could go to the Ethical Ring level and give their wealth away in order to attain spiritual enlightenment.

There are two other characteristics of a Master that are worth mentioning. The first is that a Master can laugh at himself. When a person moves to a position of observing themselves, they can see their involvement in the games as the amusement it is. The Master can laugh at his actions, feelings, the way he thinks, the objects of his games, or the way he perceives everything, especially when he gets caught up in a game he didn't know he was playing. He can laugh because he knows he is just playing.

Another important aspect to remember is the ability to improvise. If a game unfolds and a person is not ready, they have the capability to create an appropriate action. This becomes necessary quite often because they are focused on one particular game and another game unfolds simultaneously, requiring the creation of a response to the second game. Sometimes these actions may be in the form of a stalling tactic to delay the unfoldment process until we have time to focus on the new game and derive a correct action.

The initiate increases the level of fun and intensifies the game by additional risk taking. The greater the risk, the greater the challenge, and therefore the more we can experience. One may constantly appear to lay everything on the "line" to make the game more interesting and to define the boundaries of the paradigm. To the non-initiate the concept of risk increases fear and adrenaline production, but once the boundaries of a game are defined, risk is not fearful, but enjoyable. We can not lose anything of value or for that matter, receive anything of value. It is just a game. At the extreme, it could be a life and death situation, or it could be as minor as asking a person of the opposite sex for a date.

The initiate knows that there is one certainty in life, change is inevitable. What may appear today as a major risk, may tomorrow be a minor one, or visa-versa. The rules of the game remain stationary, but the aspects of every game change constantly. If the game never changes, then the players become stagnant.

This is what happens within most failing marriages and partnerships: the game becomes stagnant, primarily because one or both partners fall into a comfortable, security-oriented position. With this, there is no risk or challenge. The games that stay the same day in and day out offer no growth. Especially when the rules to a game are understood, a tendency toward stagnation occurs. Because we understand the games we don't think we have to play anymore. We had to move to the observer role to learn the rules and, from a safety position, we prefer to stay there. Knowing the rules and not playing is a total waste of time and leads to much unhappiness.

Risk, then, is really a process of experimentation through which we learn about our attachment to the concepts we place value on. These concepts include our work ethic, our self-importance, or the soundness of a relationship. Risk allows us to test the integrity of the bonds with which we hold onto these things. The true risk taker starts with the things most valuable. Through this we learn that once we put them on the "line" they no longer have any value. If we risk something, it has changed in its importance. All the tools we thought were necessary in order to play become meaningless.

Once all of our tools, the things we think necessary, have been risked and evaluated, we will see that all along we were really playing a different game than we originally thought we were because our paradigm has shifted. The real game usually is designed for one reason—so we can find happiness. We go through rigorous discipline, the great traumas, and the great unhappiness to find this elusive happiness.

Another aspect of every game is that it is always connected somehow to an "if only." "If only I could have a lot of money, then I could be ..." or "if only I could find a partner, then I could.... "

Usually we must go through the act of risk taking before we know what our real "if only" is. The "if onlys" help us define the object of our game and what our real purpose is in playing it.

Happiness is only found through play. Those that take the games seriously are by and large not happy. Granted, they may be enjoying the heaviness, but they are not happy. Generally their "if only" is "if only I could get to the end point, then I could be happy." They get so involved with the result, they forget to play. The only thing of any importance is to play with our games, and we do that by seeing them for what they are and by "being present."

The novice chess player, who says "if only I were a Master chess player, then I could really enjoy this game," or the spiritual devotee who says "if only I could reach enlightenment, then I could really be happy," are missing out in life. Their "if onlys" have destroyed their ability to play.

When the initiate changes his "if only" to a "what if," he will be able to change his focus on the game and see its many facets. What would happen to a spiritual devotee who asked, "What if I was enlightened"? Or if the novice chess player was to ask, "What if I was a Master chess player, what move would I make right now"?

And instead of saying "If only I was God, then I could change the world into a better place," we would ask, "What if I was God; what would I do right now to change the course of the world?" The "what if" statement automatically changes the focus of the game. Focus brings with it the probability of an action today, instead of a dream of tomorrow. Or worse, the "if only" causes us to whine and allows us to pretend we don't have what we want.

The "what ifs" allow us to focus on any game through any perspective. If, for instance, we are worried about world hunger, we might ask "What if I was President, what would I do for them?" Or even a better question would be "What if I was starving in some 'underdeveloped' country, what would I do then?" By asking questions like this, we view the problem through someone else's eyes. Once that happens, then we might be able to create an action to improve the situation. On the other hand, if we were to say "If only those people had money, then they wouldn't be starving," we would have a petty answer to a major problem with a solution way off in the distance. The difference in this case between the two concepts is the asker's ego. The "what if" allows him the opportunity to truly help, while the "if only" satisfies his ego that he is, in fact, a superior person. One provides a practical answer, while the other offers a theoretical one.

The use of the "what ifs" also become a necessary part in any game playing in that it enables us to know the potential moves and counter-moves of the other players. It allows us to gain potential options of ways the game can move, thereby eliminating any major surprises.

Without the Precision Ring, all of the other Rings develop into games that verify our separation from God. The Ethical Ring creates games around pseudo-mysticism, superstition, or even the reaching for personal salvation. The Conscious Ring and the Survival Ring create games around looking for external miracles or pseudo-occultism. The Mental Ring creates games around scholasticism or, at the best, metaphysics.

The initiate plays the games and participates in his activities without thought of the results. Results are secondary to his or her activities, instead of taking him or her mentally to an elusive end-point. He or she remains solely interested in his or her participation and knows that results will automatically happen. The Tao says that results will always happen because that is the natural way.

A common mistake is made when we assume mastership gives us control of the end results. Looking for results actually takes us past the game to its end, and then we miss the fun of the game and usually end up disappointed because the results did not happen the way we imagined.

The Precision Ring Masters appear to have great psychic ability because they seemingly can see the future, but usually their predictions and foresight come because of experience in a particular game. There are points when a certain move offers a predictable counter-move. Because the games are dynamic, we never know for sure which way they are moving until the next move is made. If we predict the right move, then we may be considered a mystic. If it was the wrong move, then we may be considered an impostor.

Predicting the next move is defined as a process called "Intuition." Intuition is a result of becoming one with the game. We know the game, the opponents, and the rules so well, that we can use all of this information to derive a logical guess based on how we feel the game is flowing.

It can also be a wild guess influenced by a specific result we want to attain. In this case, our intuition becomes true after much effort toward selling our belief to the other players. In other words, we influence the next move to coincide with the result we want.

We have stated that the electron ring in our model is outside the body, therefore, when we focus on this ring we move, basically, beyond the physical. We have discussed the art of observing ourselves in action, which can only happen by watching ourselves from outside of ourselves.

The other part of being outside of ourselves is an introduction to the mysteries of nature. A fantastic transformation happens when we attain mastery of this level. We develop a new sense called by many "unified thought." The first stage of unified thought includes communication with the world of nature, including animals (mammals, reptiles, fish, and insects) and the plant kingdom. This goes beyond just knowing when a plant is thirsty or a dog is hungry. This is actual mind-to-mind communication. It entails talking to a plant to discuss its history, its healing properties, food value, and even trivial things like the weather. In some instances, we may choose to see the world through the eyes of an animal, fly like an eagle, or run like a cat. The Shamans concentrate on this form of communication, but Shamanism, to most, is just another religion of the Ethical Ring.

As we grow to understand this communication process, we learn many new things. For instance, if we become ravaged by a group of mosquitoes and they annoy us, all we have to do is communicate with them on the mental level to leave us alone. We simply tell them we don't feel like playing. If they persist, we then have the option of communicating with the chief of their "tribe," and asking him to help. Usually this is as far as we need to go, but there are several levels of bosses higher than him, so we can proceed on up the ladder until we either get the results we desire or understand why things can't be changed.

It is important to remember that the kingdoms of nature respond to man one hundred percent of the time out of love, just as every other aspect of God responds out of love at all times. Is it possible that a mosquito will bite us because he loves us? Or a wild bear will attack us out of love for us?

One of the first things we learn as we enter into these mysteries is that everything in the universe has a "pecking order." Everyone has a boss, so to speak. As we work our way up the ladder of "bosses" we eventually find a group basically beyond the nature kingdoms. These are called "Nature Spirits" and include fire sprites, fairies, water nymphs, and elves. Each of these groups have many "tribes" with jurisdiction over specific classes within the nature kingdom.

These spirits are great game players. They love to tease and have fun, and they represent true mastery over the Precision Ring level. If the initiate is looking for a role-model, he or she will undoubtedly find the perfect one in this spirit kingdom.

Which brings up an interesting phenomena relative to this Ring. There are those who have read the last few paragraphs and become troubled, because they might have thought that a book of this scope shouldn't include such superstitious things as elves and fairies. Within the realm of "normal behavior," if we hear someone talking about, or even seeing, a nature spirit, we might classify them as crazy, and according to normality standards, they would be correct. However, since the Precision Ring initiate has had to shift his awareness beyond his normal body, he or she no longer fits in the category of "normal." Moving our awareness beyond our physical body implies a rearrangement of consciousness. When this rearrangement happens by a "fluke" of nature, without the understanding of this model, we will undoubtedly end up in a mental hospital. When it happens as a natural evolutionary process in conjunction with this model, we become a Master.

For instance, is a person born with the label of "retarded" a "fluke of nature"? Again, from a deterministic standpoint, this person has chosen to enter our earthly activities on the Precision Ring level with no background experiences of the four basic Rings. In other words, they chose to experience awareness without the normal mental tools or experiences necessary to operate within the basic Rings. To date, the most effective therapy for these people is to teach them basic Survival Ring skills. The concepts involved in the other three Rings are seemingly beyond their understanding. This is true of anyone who enters an exclusive Ring. Like the child genius in science or music, or the person who devotes their whole life to one Ring, they are usually dysfunctional in the other Rings.

Along the same lines, last night I took my four-year-old granddaughter, Andrea, for a walk. As we walked, I kept mulling so many things over and over in my mind, until my attention all of a sudden focused on Andrea. She was just walking along experiencing the walk as a walk, no more and no less. She just looked at and absorbed everything with no judgment and no past memory or future clouding her mind. She was in a state of total awareness and I was in an opposite place.

In Eastern terminology, they call this shift in awareness "Kundalini." Likewise, in all teachings involving Kundalini, it is preached over and over again that the movement of Kundalini without proper training is very dangerous. Proper training includes mastery over a game. Many people think that a Kundalini shift could be the answer to their prayers, a short-cut to mastery. It is not.

The Kundalini game is a fun one because of all the mystery involved. It is defined as a mysterious energy symbolized by a snake rising out of the lower Chakras to the higher ones. Not only is it a snake, but a deadly one. And in many respects the concept is true. If an awareness shift becomes a sought after result without Precision Ring, the snake will eventually turn around and attack, and send us into a neurosis or psychosis.

In conclusion, the initiate of this level of Ring is primarily interested in observing, changing, and enjoying his or her Karma. Many metaphysicians talk about karma as an inherent problem we are born with: the result of an action that happened in a previous lifetime that has come back to haunt us. We hear thousands of stories of why a particular thing is happening to a person because of their karma. "I am poor because I stole in my last life." "My husband beats me because I beat him in my last life." "My daughter torments me because she was my mother in our last life and I tormented her." Using this interpretation Karma becomes a mysterious force that hangs like a cloud over a person causing havoc and trouble.

This definition of Karma represents a great excuse for people who are not willing to learn the rules to the game. Karma is just the Eastern term for environment, i.e., the people, places, and events that currently surround us. Karma is really another way of defining the current game we are playing. In other words, we choose our karma; it is not something forced upon us. In fact, the karma we are participating in today is here because of a secret fantasy game we thought of yesterday. This game is established by our thoughts, feelings, and actions of yesterday. We have created today exactly what we wanted yesterday.

The initiate also understands that for the sake of continuity in this world, the subconscious (unconscious) minds of people within the normal spectrum of awareness automatically establish their Karma with very little input from the conscious mind. Because these games happen on a subconscious level, these people continue to play predictable games all their lives. This is explained in the *Bible* in 2 Peter 3:4. *For since the fathers fell asleep, all things continue as they were from the beginning of the creation.*

This leads the initiate to understand an important rule. He or she cannot change today's Karma, but they can only change tomorrow's. To do this, the initiate must move to consciously change his karma' providing he or she wants to. The steps are simple. First he must identify the game he is playing and make a decision to change it. He could make a wholesale change, but usually he will find there are just a few certain aspects to the present game he or she doesn't like. Second, he must decide how to play the game differently. Third, he must remember that he is now playing a self-created game, not one that was imposed upon him or her from some outside, mystical force. Thusly, he creates a new game at his discretion. Fourth, he must realize it is just a game and has no bearing on his love for himself or anyone else. And finally, he must look at what thoughts, feelings, or actions feed into the game in its present form and then change them to allow for the new rules.

As a general rule, the only reason an initiate would try to change his or her game would be if he or she was learning how to change the control of his or her games from his or her subconscious to his or her conscious mind. Conscious control of our karma (environment) is one thing that gives us the freedom so sought after.

If we redefine "Karma" as "environment," then there is no such thing as "bad karma" or, for that matter, "good karma." Karma is just Karma. The terms good and bad apply only as a judgment and are result-oriented. If the game is not producing the results we expected, then we label it as "bad karma." If we understand the rules and are enjoying the game, then it becomes "good karma."

This Ring is the first of the spiritual three that requires us to move our thinking to a place of non-judgment. This is not a discipline we need to learn; it happens almost by accident. When we understand that everyone has created their own environment down to the last stitch, that each has chosen which Ring they want to be in, and their specific personalized games, how can we judge them? Do we judge them just because they have a different agenda than we do? Granted their lives may be under the control of their subconscious, but it is still their choice to participate. Instead of judging, it would be more productive if we helped them play. The only way a person can move to conscious control is for them to hit bottom, and this is accomplished by intensifying their game, taking them to an outer limit of their paradigm.

I wouldn't do this, but as an example, what would happen if we borrowed a "homeless person's" only blanket; would that intensify their game? What if our child was disrupting our home and so we kicked them out into the street; would that intensify their game? What if we went to church and heard the minister telling the congregation that we were all headed for hell, and we started to laugh?

We must be careful, because there is a fine line between being destructive and being a Precision Ring initiate.

# Chapter 10
## Christ-Realized Ring

To attain Christhood status requires mastery over the games as well as mastery over awareness. We must be able to merge both concepts into one powerful force, and it is this action that is involved with Christhood. We mentioned earlier that we learn the rules to the game by discovering its contrasts. Whenever we can pull the power from two seemingly opposing forces by melding them together, we create a certain power separate from and yet the same. As a rough example, when male and female unite, a new force is born: a child. Separate, yet the same.

In our discussion of the Precision Ring level, we noticed that our Quantum Theory analogy was becoming less and less applicable. The electron rings demonstrated the fact that we could observe from outside the body, but they failed to show the interplay between Precision Ring and all the other Rings.

This is a common dilemma as we enter into Christhood. The easy definitions and analogies that apply at the physical levels seem to become inappropriate as our awareness changes. When we are the sun, it becomes difficult to understand why we used to pretend we were the moon. As the moon, we circled the Earth (physical) every month. However, as the sun, the Earth and moon circle us every year. The point to this analogy is that focusing on different aspects causes our awareness of reality to also change. We also find that concepts such as time and space are different. We may recognize this as the Theory of Relativity as applied to consciousness.

This is not important other than to illustrate the fact that as our focus changes, so does our perception of the world. It is very easy to see we can change our games and our definitions simply by changing our focus. In fact, the ability to change our focus is really the only thing we really have control of in this world. Definition is always a direct function of our point of focus.

As we look at the people involved in the different Rings, we see that they operate their lives by guidelines mandating a certain definition and focus. If their focus was different, they would be in another Ring and a new environment. It could be no other way. Each game within a Ring can be represented as a box or multifaceted container, depending on the complexity of the particular game, where each face of the box represents a rule or definition, and as such, represents a self-imposed limit for ourselves. (I warned you in Chapter One that we would eventually switch from never-ending circles to boxes. So here we go with what I fondly call the "Box Theory").

When all the sides of our particular box are defined and understood, we become a Master of that box. Most people have many such boxes they are trying to define, and most create obstacles to prevent them from fully disclosing those boxes to themselves and others. Without the ability to focus, there exists the probability of becoming confused and mixing up the boxes— as we try to put lid A on box B. Keeping the boxes in order and defining all sides is the responsibility of the Precision Ring initiate.

Once one box is fully defined and mastered, the initiate can move into initiate training for Christhood. This initiate looks at all the boxes he has created and redefines them by enlarging his focus. His job, if you will, is to find a box that contains all of his or her little boxes. This process requires knowledge of the games, rule definition, increased awareness, and a change in his focus. This sounds a lot more complicated than it really is. This would be easier to understand if we break down the components of a box as regards our newly developed box theory.

Picture a rectangular box. Every box has a base which represents its foundation: the base concept or belief from which the box is built.

The box has sides that contain our beliefs. These sides represent our self-imposed limits and define our beliefs relative to current awareness. The box has a top that provides us with an upper limit. Note that in our rectangular box, the top of the box (upper-limit) is the same size as the base, implying the upper-limits are directly proportional to the basic principles comprising our box's foundation.

Although we play seemingly similar games with other people, we only participate to the extent that our walls and top will allow. To increase participation is to redefine a new box.

When we dream of a new way of life, the dream usually means opening the lid to our box. We know if we can break out through the lid, a whole new world will open up to us. Yet our "real" world requires us to focus on the sides of the box for our "survival." The world we perceive as real is created by focusing inside the box. We may also strive to change the game by changing the rules, but the size of the box is always solely dependent on the size of its top and bottom.

To change our boxes, then, the first step must be to literally throw away every concept or belief that we cling to. What we perceive as truth is what defines the bottom (the foundation) of the box.

The Master realizes everything that was considered by him to be truth was colored by his focusing on the walls of his box, not necessarily on the "real" truth. As the Master looks through all his boxes, he or she will find they are all built around a supposed truth. For every truth, we find a limiting box. Since there can only be one truth, each box represents a separation of truth. Therefore, if we find the one truth, we only have one box, which is our ultimate goal at this level.

For example, through the ages the question has arisen "Who am I?" It is generally accepted in most circles that our "I" is held somewhere within our body. If that is true, then our body is a box. Look at all the ways we define this box. We see with our eyes, hear with our ears, walk with our feet, think with our brain, and so on. All of these represent sides to our box. We believe so much in the reality of our box, that we think without the sides we would not be normal, and without the box itself, we would cease to exist. Is that the truth, or is that just the way the scenario was laid out when we were born? Yet, we have read stories of people who have powers beyond what we see ranging from being a star athlete to literally walking on water. How can this be? The only way to understand this is they have somehow defined their box differently than we have.

To show how we can quickly redefine most of the concepts we have already discussed by changing our focus, let's put all our work so far into terms relating to this box theory. What would happen if instead of defining the Rings or games as electrons swirling around, we defined them as the four sides of one major box? Let's consider that one side is the Survival Ring, another is the Ethical Ring, and so on, with the bottom of our box being the belief that we are God, but we are pretending that we are not. Then, what would the upper-limit be?

If we consider this box to be based on truth, we see that the majority of people play their games by focusing on just one side of the box. For example, the Precision Ring initiate tries to master one side of the box and then tries to apply those rules to one of the other three. The Christ initiate is happy, because he now has only one box.

If we were to focus our attention on one wall of this all-encompassing universal box, we see that it is comprised of many smaller boxes running the length and width of the wall. As we look at the people playing along the wall, it appears that most of them see one tiny little box and think it is the whole wall or even the big box. There is a natural desire to master one little box, thinking that with mastery of one little box will come great power. If we step back and observe the big box, we see how small our little box really was.

If the world's population was put into a box, we would picture the walls covered with people like hungry ants at a picnic. We would see millions of people playing along the walls. As we look at this box covered with people, we could conceivably ask, "Where does freedom lie in this whole scenario?" The only place of escape, it seems, would be in the center of the box where it is still and quiet.

What happens when we move to the center of the box? Obviously, the first thing we would see is the whole box. Our awareness has, indeed, shifted. Second, we see the nonimportance of the little boxes. In the silence of the center, as we further examine the box, we begin to understand the mystery of life. The mystery that we have been looking for all along is how to get out of the box and experience the freedom that lies beyond. In our own way, that is what we are all looking for. Everyone climbing the walls is desperately trying to regain their freedom. However, if we spend our life climbing the walls, even if we make it to the top, we will still be stopped by the lid. So what is the answer?

Again, we find the need to sit back and observe the happenings within the box. As we watch, we start to laugh. We see some people working very hard to conquer one of their small little boxes, but just as they are ready to master it, they stop, retreat, and run across the wall to another box. Then we see other people who are very comfortable in their box, and they don't move at all. We also see some very enterprising people who try to use the leverage of the corners to work their way up to the top. They try to maintain a foothold in two different Rings simultaneously. Finally we see those who have made it to the top and realize they are still blocked.

As we look at the people on the walls of the box, we see that most are extremely frustrated. They are searching very hard for something, but most of them do not know what it is. They have an innate drive within themselves to search for freedom and happiness. Don't they know they won't find it in the boxes?

However, we also see some people who are really having fun. They are checking out the boxes but really not searching for anything. They join someone in their search but end up just teasing them and playing along with them. They know that freedom is just outside the box, but they have resigned themselves to the fact that the box is too secure to get out of. So they just play, hoping against all odds that maybe someday they will find a crack or a hole in one of the walls or that they will be transported from the box by a mysterious force called "Divine Grace." They have found a sense of freedom, and as such, enjoy the adventures of the small boxes and the other people they meet on the wall. These are the Precision Ring initiates.

Are they right? Is this the only choice we really have? After all, doesn't this big box represent life as we all know it? Is understanding the big box what all this is about? Wouldn't the world be a better place if all the desperate people on the walls would just realize there is no other place to go and that this is all there is?

Accepting the big box as all there is may be all right for some people, but as long as we have a drive for total freedom, we need to figure out some way to move beyond the walls and the box. How do we do that? We have already been given the answer. The box is only in existence because of our definition. Therefore, by altering that definition it will change. The reality of the big box comes into existence in the same way the smaller boxes do. The big box is based on what we think is truth.

As we sit and contemplate the big box that traps us in silence, we will also discover that no matter how we define truth, another box will be the result. This presents a major problem in our logic process. We can change our concept of truth, but it will have no effect other than to alter the box. The problem of getting free from a box will always exist.

Again, we must return to the basic premise that our interpretation of truth defines the box. Therefore, maybe we need to rethink what truth is. We see truth as something that changes relative to our individual boxes. Each box in each wall is based on a self-interpreted truth. Each wall or Ring is based on a truth. And, of course, the big box of the Christ level is also based on a truth. The boxes and the truths are considered as reality. Since we consider reality to be something tangible, we can define reality, truth, and our box by using nouns.

What would happen to our boxes if we defined reality as a verb instead of a noun? Tangible things around us would then become fluid instead of solid. Our boxes instead of being solid would become non-solid. The foundation of our boxes, truth, would become a dynamic flow of energy. What happens when we have a fluid, moving foundation? When solid foundations of our boxes disappear, our boxes become basically non-existent.

Let's look at some examples. Many people define God as a noun. With a definition like this, we see how a box is automatically created. The walls of a box automatically form surrounding our definition of God. Each wall represents a different facet of how we define God. The walls, for instance, could become the exercise of Survival Ring, reading the *Bible*, prayer, meditation, or even the belief that God is our father. The top of the box represents right action and, in this case, we ask ourselves, "How does God want me to respond in each game of the wall?"

On the other hand, if we see God as a verb, an action, no box can be built. We live our lives within the fluid nature of God. We have no box, so we have total freedom.

Another example is that the science of physics has shown light into two defined boxes. We find, however, that depending on the particular box we try to put "light" into, we will get different definitions. One box says light is a wave and the other claims it is a particle. Both are correct, based on the truth of the individual experiments. However, again, if light is a verb, then neither definition is viable. Light as a verb represents the action of adding energy to a system.

Since, according to physics, every action has an equal and opposite reaction, if we interpret light to be a verb, then we must also assume darkness is a verb. The discussion of light verses dark is widely used in most spiritual discourses, giving them names: light is God and dark is Satan. As verbs, these opposing definitions become non-existent and are an interplay between two types of motion, which takes away our desire for attachment, since we can not own a verb. Many spiritual people reach for the light and dream of becoming enlightened. This is a natural response to a noun, ownership. If only they would concentrate on lighting the world or lightening their life (i.e., turning on the light in their box), they would be happier. In contrast, many spiritual practices are performed in the dark. In the darkness, we find great spiritual power primarily because of the uninterrupted clarity that avails itself. Darkness brings with it peace, serenity, rest, and no interruptions—at least conceptually.

Both light and dark are extremes. As in every case we have discussed so far, we first must explore the extremes and then find a middle ground. We can gain great spiritual insight by finding the area where the motion of light meets the motion of darkness and emerging ourselves in contemplation and meditation. Nature provides two times a day when this happens: dawn and dusk. Both represent a time when spiritual energy is stronger. Another spiritual exercise that provides the same effect is when we light a candle in the dark. The light of the candle in the dark room gives us a very definite contrast. Power comes where the darkness meets the light.

When we learn to shift our awareness to the point where two opposing motions meet, we see that a vortex is created at that point. It is through these vortexes that great learning and new experiences happen. For example, astral travel and astral projection happen when the action of sleep meets the action of being awake. Some scientists and most science fiction writers believe that black holes (vortexes) are created when one universe meets another.

To take this one step further, when we contemplate our lives in the future, we dream about tomorrow's actions. Very seldom, if at all, do we look into the future and see a still picture. Rather, we always see tomorrow as a verb describing future actions. We also see how yesterday describes past actions. Very seldom do we project ourselves into the future or past in the form of definition, it is almost always as a verb. We also know that many of us explore the future and past on a constant basis. When we do this, we are experiencing two opposing verbs. Again, the Master wants to be in the middle, not in one of the extremes. Where the action of tomorrow meets the action of yesterday is called the action of today. This vortex called "now" is represented by almost all Masters and teachings as a very spiritual place.

We see that within the verb concept everything is action. The only time frame available for an action to happen is right now. We can take this a step further. When we experience and focus our attention within the now, we find that at that point, time does not exist. In fact, time is only relative as a difference between future and past. Since there is a direct relationship between time and space, we will also find that space becomes non-existent, bringing with it more intrigue.

The following story gives us a different slant on this concept:

## The Sacrifice

Zen Master Charlie was in his usual resting place high atop his favorite mountain, Mount Charlie. At this point, no one knew if Mount Charlie was named after Zen Master Charlie or if it was the other way around. The quiet environment of the mountain gave Charlie much time to think, meditate, commune with God, and devise many Zen parables and answers to many daily problems. To visit Zen Master Charlie was to first become humble with Mount Charlie's majesty, and to visit Mount Charlie was to feel the wisdom of Zen Master Charlie. The mountain and the master worked hand in hand; one wouldn't be the same without the other. They lived in beautiful harmony.

As Charlie grew spiritually, and actually approached the God-level of existence, he saw that becoming one with God is actually to become one with everything in the universe. As he looked at the structure of man and all things, he saw that they all have a common point where they meet and become one. It is demonstrated in the way Mount Charlie was formed. There are many rocks at its base building towards a peak. Yet, he knew that all the rocks were still a part of Mount Charlie and all were a part of God.

Through this great wisdom, he surmised that the total of everything equals God. In other words, God is the sum total of all his parts. Mathematically this is expressed as:

$$\textbf{YOU + ME + THEM + IT + ..... = GOD}$$

Once Zen Master Charlie arrived at this final conclusion, he became very disappointed and went into an extreme state of depression. He realized that because he had reached a summation, for him to grow meant that another part of the sum had to wither. This meant that he had achieved his masterhood at a cost to someone else. Since energy can neither be created nor destroyed, the energy that he put forth in his search for truth had to be taken from someone else. He had required so much energy to reach the level he was at that it might mean that at this very moment someone, somewhere in the universe was lying on his deathbed from a lack of energy.

Being the loving, compassionate man Charlie was, he decided to commit the greatest sacrifice he could and perform the greatest deed, the greatest kindness to society in general and specifically to this man on his deathbed. So off the mountain Charlie jumped to his death: a state of being that requires no energy. All the energy he had acquired could then be used and shared by many others to help them attain mastery after his death.

The world mourned Charlie's death. Charlie awoke from his death as a pure energy form. "What have I done?" he thought to himself. I was going to spread my energy, my life force, throughout the world and yet it seems I am still requiring energy—maybe even more now than before. "What have I done?"

As Charlie looked back at Earth, he was also shocked to see no difference. It seemed everyone was still the same and, in fact, people were still dying from a lack of energy. Charlie was disappointed, for it seemed his sacrifice was of no benefit at all. In truth, it seemed the world was more confused because he was no longer there to help those that came to him. Even Mount Charlie was not the same anymore.

Charlie was upset, and he wandered around for a while (for some reason his watch stopped ticking, so we don't know how long he was wandering) until he saw a high, beautiful mountain. It looked like Mount Charlie, but it was also in its pure energy form just like Charlie. Not knowing what else to do, he ascended to the top of the mountain to continue his contemplation and commune with God. And so there he sat, working through his thoughts and, in so doing, increasing his energy.

"Why didn't my theory work ?" he wondered. "Is there something wrong with my mathematical model?" Yet he knew that wherever there is an apparent contradiction, the initial premise must be incorrect. As he thought back to his initial premise, he discovered what was wrong. The answer was simple, and he really knew it all the time.

Man perceiving the world through his biological make-up, sees an image and feeds that image into his brain by transforming it according to his perception, and in so doing, he creates the different parts of God. Since we are transforming these parts to make things easier to understand, all the parts are, in essence, an illusion. Therefore, since there are no parts, there can be no sum of the parts; there is only God.

Zen Master Charlie left the mountain that day wanting to learn more about this illusion. He wondered if maybe there were other aspects of God he had not yet experienced, now that he truly realized he was everything.

Unfortunately, it was too late, he had already left the Earth-plane, or had he?

# Chapter 11

## God-Realized Ring

The final step in our model is the process of creation; after all isn't that what Gods do, create? If we thought about it, and if we could create whatever we wanted, then wouldn't we be totally free? I mean, if I wanted to be alone and created my own planet or universe and lived on it by myself, isn't that freedom? If we wanted to experience total power and created a life where everyone worshipped us constantly, isn't that freedom?

Freedom is a process whereby we have complete conscious control over our environment and actions. The key word is conscious: it has come up before in our discussion.

This Ring—the God-Realized Ring—pertains specifically to God realization, which relates to the most basic of the concepts we have talked about so far. In my dream, we saw that as the different heavens were created, they became more complex, with the Survival Ring being the most complicated. Therefore, it stands to reason that if we reverse the process, they should become simpler and more encompassing. The primary concept to master in this Ring is consciousness, which includes an awareness of everything there is to know about all the Rings we have discussed so far. We have called it "mastery" before, but it is more than that, it is becoming one with everything.

We have discussed many concepts so far to show us how to play, how to change our awareness and our focus, and how to identify where we are, but we haven't yet uncovered how all of this is created.

We have also mentioned that if we don't consciously create our environment we will automatically do it unconsciously. This level requires conscious responsibility for everything that happens in our lives, which, in turn, creates a spiraling effect through the world and universe. So let's talk some more about this creative process.

Most of us at specific times in our lives want the ability to consciously create. This usually happens when we are frustrated with the way our life is.

We generally experience something we don't like, or we don't feel we are moving out of our endarkenment fast enough. If we are poor, we want to manifest riches; if we are sick, we want to manifest health. The real problem is that we are involved in a game, and through our judgment process we feel as if we are losing. Basically, what we want to do is change the game.

When faced with this dilemma, we must realize that without a shift in awareness, all we usually do is just switch games. Moving out of one game into another does not mean we can leave our problems behind nor does it mean we move to a place where games don't exist. We must remember our sole job is to master whatever game we are in. Sure, we can focus on another game for awhile, but whenever we turn around, our previous game will hit us in the face again. It may have different players, but the game will be the same. I have had several times in my life when I noticed I was reliving a part of my life I thought I had finished. For instance, I have a step-son by my previous marriage who was going through the throes of alcoholism/drug addiction, and I felt I had resolved my problems around it, only to find myself remarried and going through the same process again with both of my new step-children.

So since we apparently have no choice about the game we choose to play, we need to look at the possibility of changing the game by using our creative powers to get us through the game faster or at least with some control on our part. We are trying to reform the game from within. This is one type of creation.

The environment we are involved in is usually set up on an unconscious level, which is relatively easy to understand, since we can somewhat see how our subconscious can dictate where and how we live or our actions. What is more difficult to understand is how the players are chosen. The process is simple when we think in terms of everyone on the planet being connected through the universal mind. When we decide what game to play and what we want to experience from that game, we send that game plan out to everyone in the universe via our universal mind connection. Everyone receives our thought transmission simultaneously, and those that want to play show up all of a sudden. Without knowledge of this model, we call this either luck or fate, but it is a situation previously agreed upon by both parties. If I want to get married and experience the process of being afraid of my spouse, then someone will come to fulfill that fantasy for me. Emerson says,

> *Nature is always consistent though she feigns to contravene her own laws. She keeps her laws, and seems to transcend them. She arms and equips an animal to find its place and living in the earth, and, at the same time, she arms and equips another animal to destroy it . (Emerson, Emerson's Essays. 1926, p.389)*

We are all God and we respond one hundred percent of the time out of love. People come into our lives and do all sorts of things with and to us, play all sorts of games with us, for one reason: because they love us. People also cheat, lie, manipulate, abuse, be kind, give us money, or any number of other things because they love us enough to help us create our perfect fantasy, no matter how sick it might be.

We can change the game consciously by creating a new fantasy. We do this by first discovering what our present fantasy is. What rewards are we currently deriving from our game? If we could change the game, how would we change it? Most of us have heard this question many times at any number of prosperity or goal setting workshops. Within these classes, we see some people who seem to use the principles and get them to work in their lives, while many more can't seem to apply them.

The biggest enemy we have is our rationalization process. We must first admit, before anything else can be done, that the emotions we are experiencing are true feelings. When we admit that we are in pain or hurt or broke, we move from rationalization to honesty. The natural tendency is to rationalize these things and say they are for our own good, or "This is my Karma," or some other reason that takes us out of the now into the future or past. It doesn't mean that we must live with suffering, but we can't change it if we don't first acknowledge its presence. Pretending it does not exist is a game within itself. We must also realize these feelings are not good or bad, they just are. We created each game to learn something, but that does not mean we need to get stuck in any particular game.

The problem with setting goals is that most people try to set goals using nouns. Those that are successful using goal setting principles, set their goals using verbs. Each goal becomes an action in the future. In other words, if we are playing the financially poor game, we might set our goal as having lots of money, a new car, a new house, or some other noun. We do all the necessary mental work and then passively sit around waiting for our goal to manifest. What are the odds that it will happen?

But what happens if we see that we are playing the financially poor game and realize what we would really like is a job that would allow us to be involved in a world-wide project that would greatly help humanity? The odds for change are in our favor because we are looking for action. If we then get a call from the President of the United States asking us to become his Secretary of State, would our financial problems be solved? The point is, it is easier for the other Gods in this world to approach us and say let's play, than for them to arbitrarily walk up to us and hand us a hundred dollar bill.

We don't play our games to confirm that the world is a noun, we play them as a way to allow us the experiences of different actions that this particular form allows. Therefore, we don't directly want to manifest certain things, as much as we want to manifest certain responses from the other players.

So the part of the creative process we initially want to gain control of is the process of receiving desired responses. We do not gain control by manipulating our current environment, i.e., our friends, family, current job, etc. To control our responses we need to control our unconscious; we do this by becoming conscious. People are generally unhappy in their current games because their actions seem to be limited. Because their environment is dictated by their subconscious, they have limited freedom to move-they are limited by their perception of their environment. If a person is currently living on the street and needs money, his actions are rather limited as to how he can acquire money, as well as how much he can receive at one time. He can get money by begging, stealing, or as a day laborer. For him to receive a large amount of money would require him to change his environment.

A great fallacy in normal thinking comes to light when we view the term "action" as strictly a physical response, i.e., hard work is the key to success. When we observe the truly great players, they use much more mental action than physical. In fact, the art of mastership is really one of mental gymnastics. Someone once said that success is ninety percent perspiration and ten percent inspiration. I believe it is not physical perspiration, but rather mental perspiration. Inspiration is the start of the creative process; it is the answer to our question of how we want to change our environment.

Once we decide on a specific response (inspiration) we want to manifest, we then send out a mental request to all the other players in the universe. Those who want to play our "new" game will come to us. Very quickly, a new environment will be established whereby we will be allowed to live out our new fantasy.

We send this out as an invitation, but with force behind it so the new players can be sure we will offer them a new challenging game, a game that will be more fun than their present one. The power we use to send out this invitation is called WILLPOWER.

The *Bible* explains it really well when it says that God created the heavens and the earth by the Word. Of course, like many other biblical concepts, there are many definitions of God's Word, but they are usually interpreted as either a goal, desire, incantation, conversation, or thought; it is all and yet none of these concepts.

The term "Word" is used to imply the act of using the creative power inherent within us all. Through the ages another word has come into play; it is "Will," with "Willpower" being the force behind our creative process.

A sample of an invitation would be "I am ready for (whatever action we desire) to happen now." An example would be, " I am ready for my product to be used now." If it feels better, we could also add, " I know my product will be for the betterment of mankind and I need help. I am willing to perform any actions necessary for the accomplishment of this request." We could call these invitations "affirmations"; but then they are directed out instead of being something we want to change within ourselves. Its just a matter of a different focus.

Once our invitation is formulated, we incorporate it into ourselves until we really feel like it is what we truly want to create. During this time of patient waiting, we will encounter many reasons why we really would not like it to happen. Our doubts and fears will come to the forefront, and as we face them, we must make a choice if we really want the change to happen or not. We must then allow it to swell up inside of us with a power behind it as if it is trying to escape. We then take that thought, and by using our willpower, force it out of our body into the universe. The success of this process depends on how serious we are about changing our environment as well as our power of concentration and focus. If we feel any doubt while we are doing this, we must just keep on doing it until we are sure it has been heard and believed by the other players. Once accepted by the other players, they will come to play.

The secret is to know throughout our whole body that what we desire to change has happened, not merely wished or hoped for, but we know it. The faster we come to that point of realization, the faster we can create.

The other aspect is that we don't sit around waiting. We do the activities our hands find to do each day. We do this because we don't how our creation will manifest. If we just sit, the right time for an action may pass us by and our creation will have lost its chance to come into fruition.

In ancient teachings, there are many references to the practice of silence. The creative process requires silence as an integral part of its practice. Verbally telling other people about an invitation before it is sent out and accepted depletes the power necessary to send it out.

A good analogy is a steam boiler. If we put energy (heat) into a boiler, it will build up tremendous pressure. However, if we constantly activate the pressure relief valve, it will not build up the required pressure. If the boiler was hooked up to a whistle and we let it build up enough steam, when it was the proper time, we could put out a sound that could be heard around the world.

The important thing to remember is we are only putting out the invitation. We have absolutely no control over who comes to play or how they play. It could be someone we have never met who is involved in an area we have never heard of before. One person could come or millions. However it manifests, our desire for a change in our environment will happen if we perform the right action at the right time.

By verbally extending our invitations to the people around us, we may be able to stroke our ego, but very seldom will it allow us to change our environmental actions. We all have a need to be validated, that is true, but doesn't this imply that we are wishing and hoping but not knowing? Knowing gives us automatic validation. We need to get in touch with new people who can satisfy our new fantasy, our old friends are part of our old environment. To try to bring them along with us into our new environment is self-defeating and keeps us in our old fantasy. This is the first level in the creative process: contemplate a change, then know it will happen.

We then move from the use of willpower to enthusiasm. Enthusiasm is defined as "God within." It is the power that gives our creation the impetus to get started. I am reminded of the old saying, "If we set ourselves on fire, people will come, if for no other reason than to watch us burn." I visualize this whole process like this: I send out my invitation which gets everyone's attention; they all know I am serious about it because they can tell I know it is going to happen with or without them. Then they feel the enthusiasm around my plan, and they either come to participate or come to investigate.

As an example, let's say all of a sudden out of the blue we see this beautiful picture in our mind. We decide we want to paint it; automatically the world knows we are going to paint a picture. We know, first of all, that we can paint what we saw. Secondly, we know it is something that will add beauty to the world; the world now knows we are serious. We paint our picture with enthusiasm, loving how each color blends with the next and the way we express ourselves on canvas. When we finish, we have a masterpiece, and the world knows it. Everyone can feel when such an event is happening.

A second type of creative process relates to the apparent instant manifestation of nouns: creating money instantaneously, turning water into wine, and so on. This is a much more difficult process and requires an awareness shift. In the first level of the creative process we are changing the environment. To instantaneously manifest we create changes by redefining the box.

The real key to this creative process lies in the word "apparent." The Master who can manifest items which we see as nouns is really using his willpower to combine actions, thereby creating a new action that the rest of us in normal awareness interpret as a specific noun. The master of this type of creative process sees the world as strictly a relationship of one motion combining with another motion. To more fully understand this process, let's look more closely at relationships.

As a personal note to help explain parts of this book and especially this section, I need to tell you that I consider myself to be a Zen-Taoist. Neither term, "Zen" nor "Tao," is understood very well by people not involved in these particular teachings. To many, they represent a contradiction in terms, which is the intent.

As a point of definition, Taoism is the study of contrasts of action, while Zen is the study of contrasts that exist in concept. Taoism is a left brain action, while Zen is a right brain action, to use current vernacular. Taoism practices passiveness through active action, while Zen activeness through passive action. This is not to be confused with the religious practices of Zen-Buddhism.

The Tao compliments Zen in much the same way that Christianity compliments Hinduism. Those Christians who resist the study of Hinduism are missing out on very important concepts of their religion because they do not get to experience the contrasts that Hinduism provides. The opposite is true also with the Hindus.

Although I first studied Christianity, then went to Hinduism, I left them both because I saw my newly defined Zen-Taoism offered a better base to draw resources from. In other words, it is easier for me to see how Christian-Hindu concepts are developed from my Zen-Tao principles than visa-versa. Zen-Taoism is my way of taking things to their simplest form; complexity usually only satisfies the ego, very seldom does it take us to the truth.

This has been a brief example of the relationship between one concept versus another. The study of relationships is what generally leads a Master to an ability to manifest apparent nouns in the creative process.

The basis of any relationship is a flow that exists between two or more actions. For instance, if I love you and you don't love me back, a relationship is formed. Not a very good one, but a relationship has been created. Whenever two actions come into play with each other a relationship is born, regardless of what those actions seem to be.

We have a choice in our lives to either resist relationships or accept them and allow the flow of the combining energy to take us where it wants. If we resist, we usually remain stagnant.

A relatively good example of how flow works is the weather. The study of meteorology shows that weather is moved around this world by nature, which creates low and high pressure areas. A low pressure area creates a type of vacuum to be filled by a high pressure area. Likewise, when a high pressure area moves, it is replaced by a low pressure area. The interplay between these two actions causes a flow of energy across the country that we call weather. If there was only one pressure, the weather would not change and we would become very bored, and our environment would always remain the same, at best, or deteriorate at the worst.

This is a fairly good example, because it gives us a key that enables us to determine if a flow is really happening in our lives. If a flow exists, things change. The faster the changes, the greater the flow. As we said earlier, the only way to stop a flow of energy is by resistance. We do this by building a wall either physically, mentally, or emotionally. For instance, we can build a house so we won't be affected by changes in the weather, or we can wall up a feeling so we can feel more stable. These areas represent pockets of stagnant energy where we go to hide from change; this is how we stay safe. We move to these positions and sit back on our laurels, as we watch the world go by. We resist change because we are either afraid to move in a new direction or afraid to let the winds of change take us wherever they might go. But change is what makes our lives interesting, and we all have an innate desire to make today different from yesterday. In every relationship we have, we anticipate some sort of change if we truly want a flow of energy to take place.

When we look at nature, we see the way it creates a flow of energy, and by applying this understanding to ourselves, we can learn a lot. An interesting personal example of this is when I took a hike into the mountains outside of Boulder, Colorado and planted myself next to a beautiful little stream. I found myself watching the water, and I noticed there were rocks in the stream. I decided to pretend I was a drop of water. At one point, I was a part of the whole stream flowing in unity with the rest of the water. As I approached the first rock, I was separated from the rest of the stream and forced to go on my own. Yet, later, down the stream I rejoined the main body of water. From this I learned that nothing is forever and that a feeling of separation would soon pass.

In order to understand what "flow" is, let's look again at the weather. Weather (as a concept) cannot be seen, although it does carry with it certain nouns like snow, rain, etc. Weather is strictly an action verb. We can see from nature that when we are experiencing an apparent low (or lack) that we are also surrounded by highs (fulfillment). Only by resistance to the highs will our needs not be fulfilled. Sometimes we just love the peace and tranquillity so much that we resist the activity the high will bring. Likewise, sometimes we love the activity of the high so much, we resist the movement to the low. It is not the definition of highs and lows that is really important, it is the change from one to the other and the movement that is inherently available to propagate the flow of energy.

We have discussed previously that Masters see the world as a verb. Weather is really two verbs playing off of each other. There are two types of verbs of primary concern to us: active and passive. The thing most interesting about these two types of verbs is that they both require equal amounts of energy. How could it be otherwise?

Relating this to physics, there is a similarity between the power of verbs and that of energy. Energy is divided into two types: potential (passive) and kinetic (active). Nothing moves in this world without these two forms of energy balancing, contrasting, and playing off each other. It is this relationship between passive and active energies that creates everything in the named universe. A certain percentage of active energy balanced by passive energy creates a particular relationship that can be defined as a particular noun. The relationship is simple, but it appears very complex because of the infinite numbers of possibilities; there are enough combinations available to claim that everything in this world is unique.

To relate this argument to the ideas discussed in this book, there are two complimenting actions that relate to every aspect of our lives. These are the light and dark actions of the Survival Ring, the light and dark thoughts of the Mental Ring, and the light and dark morals of the Ethical Ring. It can be broken down further by classifying light as active energy and dark as passive energy. A simple example exists in a rainbow. The higher colors which are the blues and violets have more light than dark, and the ones on the bottom( the reds) have more dark than light. Many people seek the power of the light and ignore the dark. Yet, the dark has as much power as the light. In fact, the power of the light is usually found by mastering the dark. The antithesis is also true, when one masters the light, the power of the dark is revealed.

Several religions view the darkness as evil and the light as good. Nothing could be further from the truth, as darkness represents the unknowing, while the light represents knowledge. If this concept seems questionable, then sit in a totally dark room for awhile, you will discover that nothing exists in the darkness. Things we previously knew were in the room totally disappear in the darkness. If one were to walk around a darkened room, one would surely bump into things. Our world becomes identified by our sense of touch, but what if we could not identify each object we encounter just by feeling? We would become scared, and if we became afraid enough, we would call it evil. When we become fearful we identify that part of our world which hides in the dark as evil. Is it really evil or just unknown?

The next part of this great experiment is to add light to the room. Things we bumped into in the dark now become identified and our fear leaves us. Light brings with it definition, so our quest for the light is really a quest for knowledge. The term "enlightenment" is the action of reaching out for knowledge.

This definition of enlightenment creates a contradiction in our normal thinking process because we work very hard in our lives to receive knowledge and definition; we go to school, to church, and we read and study to receive new knowledge. The only possible reason we would do these actions is if we inherently know we are in the dark. Without the darkness, the need for light would not exist. If we were totally enlightened, i.e., knew everything there was to know, what would our lives be like? Wouldn't it in some ways be comparable to living with sunshine twenty-four hours a day, all year long? It would, at the very least become very boring. Therefore, the natural process is that for every piece of knowledge there is an equal amount of unknowing. That is why knowledge changes throughout the history of man; what was considered true yesterday could become untrue today. We work hard to acquire some particular piece of knowledge, but when we get to the point where we understand it, we generally realize it is based on a lie or a half truth. Then off we go again to uncover the truth. Darkness always hides part of the truth from us. As we light up part of the darkness where we couldn't see before, we find that the basis for our argument has also changed. What we thought was true before was based strictly on how much of the unknowing we had uncovered. For instance, this book appears to me as truth, yet when I get to the point of understanding all the concepts herein written, I will see all the falsehoods incorporated within. I will do this by discovering new, unanswered questions and paradoxes. For the sake of argument, don't questions always represent the unknowing and the answer the knowledge? Neither has any purpose by itself; the only use for either one comes from the other. Questions without any hope of an answer are unnatural. Likewise, answers without questions lead to the same imbalance.

Being involved in this relationship between darkness (unknowing) and the light (knowledge) is what keeps us alive and moving. Those that see their knowledge as the only truth and don't explore it further to see if it is real, become stagnant.

Growth and change only exist through the interplay of light and dark. By accepting the unknowable as a fact that can not be changed is as detrimental to our growth as believing that truth is real. Only those who are willing to blend the two types of energy together will grow.

The early Eastern Masters understood this balance of energy. To help their students, they devised a graphic representation of it which is called the Yin-Yang symbol. The purpose of the symbol is to show the balance between light and dark. Not only does it show the primary relationship, it also shows that within the light there is dark, and within the dark there is light.

There are some who would relate this to Jesus' teachings, when He said, "I am the Way, the Truth, and the Light." Why didn't He say He was also the dark? Jesus came into this world as a teacher. Teaching is the giving of the light of knowledge. Yet, although He had the knowledge (at least metaphorically), didn't He still have to contend with darkness, which the *Bible* calls Satan? When He was confronted by Satan, what options were given to him?

Satan offered him a life of sitting back and receiving all that life had to offer (passive action). Obviously, this would be a pretty tempting choice for most of us, but Jesus opted to take the other choice: active action. That is one reason why He preached so often on the virtues of giving and loving, both are verbs of active action.

Jesus' Parables in the *Bible* show the concept of activity verses passiveness. Two good examples are the "Prodigal Son" and the "Talents." In both stories the person performing the action and activity received greater rewards than the person who performed passively. Through these teachings, we also see the contrast that exists between giving and receiving; like light and dark there maintains a balance between the two. Likewise, those that concentrate on giving without ever receiving become greatly out of balance. Many people consider giving and receiving to be separate actions, but they are not. One is active and the other is passive. By redefining the Yin-Yang symbol from light and dark to receiving and giving, we discover the true nature of these actions.

To confuse or clarify this, let's return to our initial analogy of the electron in the atom. In that analogy we made the statement that the electron becomes enlightened and moves to a higher ring when it receives light. It becomes endarkened or moves to a lower ring when it gives off light. This is an apparent contradiction; isn't giving an active action and receiving a passive action? Yet, in our electron analogy, isn't it true that the act of giving takes us into darkness and the act of receiving takes us into the light? Yes, in fact, science proves this: the amount of kinetic energy used transforms in a proportional amount to become potential energy.

Therefore, we give, teach, love, and all of our other actions to help us move into darkness (potential energy). The depth of the darkness is directly related to the height of the light. Is it possible Jesus was able to transcend death (at least metaphorically) because his life was devoted to action and to the light? Doesn't the *Bible* also tell us that during the period between his crucifixion and when he rose from the dead, that he spent three days entrenched in the deepest recesses of darkness? Was it then, with all that potential energy at his grasp, He was able to achieve total knowledge?

His knowledge of how to use light and dark could conceivably be the one main thing that set him apart from the rest of us. He obviously had a plan and was able to put it into practice in his life. He did not take these seemingly opposing forces arbitrarily.

There are many who understand the balancing effect, but do not use it to precision. They may spend their life in action by giving, but they are unable to go deeper into the darkness. They give up their power by taking tokens of appreciation. Nowhere do we see Jesus asking for material rewards or praise to compensate him for his teachings. It was just the opposite. During his <u>Sermon on the Mount</u>, the *Bible* says He gave food to all those who came. His goal was to build that potential energy inherent in each one of us. This action is what has made Jesus so widely worshipped and thought of. As a people, we always hold in high regard anyone who has explored unknown ground. This is what Jesus did according to the *Bible*. As far as we know, to date, He is the one who has experienced the deepest, darkest secrets of the unknown and came back alive. This also places him in the position of being the most knowledgeable person this universe has ever known.

Mathematically, we find that the Yin-Yang symbol represents a summation. The circle represents the total and within it we have basically two halves and two smaller circles. The summation of both halves represents the total amount of energy available. The use of the wavy line is to show that a relationship exists between the two components. In mathematics when we look at a summation equal to a constant total, we know that as one factor becomes larger, the other must become smaller. Therefore, the more kinetic energy (light) we use, the more of the circle becomes encompassed in potential energy (dark). Likewise, the more passive (dark) we become, the more activity (light) is available. As a tangible example, the more money we receive (passive), the more opportunities we have to give it away (active).

Many people jump back and forth between the two sides, never exploring the depths of either side. Within the depth of either side (shown within the symbol) lies a reason for exploring its depth. The symbol shows us that somewhere hidden in the recesses of each form of energy is a circle. Within the darkness it is a circle of light, and within the light it is a circle of darkness. These circles represent great mysteries. Within the darkness is hidden knowledge; within the light is hidden darkness, an avenue to unknown worlds.

One more point must be made about this symbol before we proceed to its application. The line that separates the two halves is the point of detachment. This line can only be achieved when both halves are experienced and understood. Many people interpret detachment as moving into the dark, because in that state they are not actively pursuing anything. They are close to understanding detachment in their practice, but obviously wrong in their interpretation. Being passive does not mean that detachment has been mastered. It just means a move that been made to the potential energy side. Detachment is the vortex created when two seemingly opposing energies come together.

There are many opinions as to what is the opposite of love. They range anywhere from fear to hatred to apathy. Love is an action verb, so the opposite must be a passive verb. For the sake of clarification, let's call the two sides "active love" and "passive love." Verbs like hatred and fear are active verbs. Granted, they represent negative action, but action is action. Apathy on the other hand is a passive verb of negative action.

These opposites in themselves create havoc with personal relationships. The insecure person who wants to be loved all the time will be greatly disappointed when the shift to the other side requires they become the lover. The shift also implies that the person who was the lover now wishes to be loved. If the other person does not change, either they both are in conflict as they try to give their love to the other without either receiving, or they become very passive towards each other. Both situations lead to troubled relationships.

The most confusing issues around personal relationships are the preconceived roles of man and woman. By nature, the male energy is said to be the active side of the relationship and the female energy is the passive side. This is a statement that both sexes will disagree with, as well they should. But predetermined roles classify the male as the one who is the provider, protector, authority for the family, and biologically during sexual intercourse, he is the giver. The female on the other hand is classified as the peace maker, nurturer, home maker and, biologically during sexual intercourse, she is the receiver.

As we know, neither description is necessarily always true, but they are roles that constantly cloud our relationship issues. So when the male moves to passive and the female sees that as an unnatural state, she revolts. And, of course, the opposite happens when the female moves to the active position.

Christianity is classified as a male religion. Therefore, the *Bible* teaches over and over again the use of male energy. It even refers to God as "He." Hinduism, on the other hand, addresses female energy in more detail. In fact, it addresses God in two parts: Father-Mother God. The religion that focuses almost exclusively on female energy is called "witchcraft." It identifies God as a female called "Isis."

If we look at the nations that have Christianity as their primary religion versus the countries that practice Hinduism, we can see these concepts in use. The Christian countries appear to be more male because they show force and aggressiveness, as they try to maintain the role of world protector. The religions of the Hindu countries, on the other hand, are thought of as very passive and try to follow Ghandi's teachings of passive resistance. The Christian countries seem to be on the leading crest of knowledge, while the Hindu countries seem to be more spiritually ritualistic. (Please excuse my pretension that these are black and white differences, but it is easier to give examples when we label concepts in separate boxes.)

To continue, relating the concept of God to the Yin-Yang symbol, Father God represents the light side and Mother God represents the dark side. It is interesting that religions which focus on just one side of the symbol, in essence, tilt the symbol on its side and see the light above the dark. The light represents something of a "higher nature" and the dark stays beneath in the form of evil or sinister ways. One example, of course, is Heaven and Hell.

We have discussed many terms that have a contrasting relationship which can be symbolized by the Yin-Yang symbol. It is important to realize that they are all just different aspects of the two primary energies: kinetic verses potential. All contrasting terms are just deviations of those energies and relate to our previous discussion of definition. To focus on one energy, and pretend it doesn't have a balancing energy of equal importance, is to forego any chance for understanding. Separation is always an illusion.

The first thing to remember is that change is a natural process. Creating change in our lives only serves to throw the energies out of balance. Yes, after all the preceding pages, which discussed how to create change, it boils down to changing the relationship between active and passive energies. Now the question arises as to whether this is something we actively need to do. If the flow has stopped in our lives, it is because we are not perceiving the changes that are happening naturally, or we are ignoring them. We need to wake up every morning knowing that our life is going to change in some way during the day, because it will change. Once the possibility of change is accepted, we need to pay attention to the changes that are taking place and move with them.

The second thing is to not judge the changes. We steer away from changes because we fear the unknown. We have no idea where each new change will take us until we proceed along the path for awhile. I remember having a meditation once where I was on a conveyor belt being transported through a tunnel. I became afraid, grabbed on to the tunnel entrance, and freed myself of the conveyor belt. Now, I will never know what I would have experienced had I just gone along for the ride.

In order to realize changes, we need to first realize where we are. It is important, upon awakening, that time be taken to clear our thoughts and actions from the night. To start fresh, we must center ourselves through a morning ritual of meditation, prayer, or contemplation. It is also recommended that a habit of journal writing be established. Putting thoughts down on paper has the therapeutic effect of releasing all those past and future thoughts and clearing them out of our heads. This process literally pulls us back into our bodies and allows us to see our environment more clearly.

It is rather difficult at times to see the changes when they first begin. As we shift our energy from one action to its contrasting action, we cross over the line that we symbolized as a vortex. When we reach the vortex, we know we are in the throes of change. At this point in our movement, we can see many options and can feel a swirling of energy. This vortex is the proper point to respond to the change and make our choices. At this point, we have some control over a responding action. If we wait until we are already involved in the other energy, then usually the course of action is limited to only a few appropriate responses. Once a change becomes apparent, we need to move with that change. This is the Precision Ring-the right action at the right time. The Precision Ring initiate looks for and resonates with the vortex because this gives us our right timing. It is also at this vortex that the Christ initiate can see the fallacy of the box. It is at this vortex that the God initiate can create a manifestation (by creating a vortex). So first we feel a change in the energy, then we see chaos happening around us as the energies from the opposing actions interweave themselves. As we approach the center of the vortex, we meet the eye of the storm (or should it be the "I" of the storm). Within the eye, everything seems peaceful and calm. This is where we perform our action, this is the right time. Once we make our action, we need to once again go through the chaos before we start our new journey, so before and after any creation there is always apparent chaos.

If we don't see or respond to changes in our lives, then by choice we are stuck. Being stuck in activity is exemplified by the person who is always busy. They may not accomplish anything, but they are always busy. It could be taking care of the house or running from one appointment to another, never allowing themselves any movement to their potential energy side. Since receiving is an aspect of potential energy, their lives seem to be lacking.

Being stuck in passivity is exemplified by the person who never does anything. They may sleep all day, read, watch television, or just wait for something to happen. They don't perform any action above and beyond survival requirements. Since giving creates the potential for receiving, they will usually experience life as lacking.

On the other hand, if we allow ourselves to experience change, we are balancing the two energies. If we respond with the proper action, then we grow and have a happy, abundant life. The correct action is always one of the opposite energy. For instance, if someone offers us money, we move to passive and receive. If someone is in need, then we give. If someone has a question, we respond with knowledge. If they have knowledge, we respond with a question. If they are hurt, we heal. If they are a healer, we show them where we hurt. If they want love, we give it. If they have love, we accept it. If they are in danger, we protect. If they can protect, then we accept their shelter. These are natural ways to respond. Similar responses are given the opportunity to occur during change.

Let's go back a little, because we also need to define right action beyond what we talked about in the Ethical Ring. In any relationship, there are two or more forces interacting upon each other. To give a response that only helps one of the parties involved and is directed at only one of the forces, is an improper response. The correct response to any change must be multidirectional with the intent to satisfy the demands of all the forces at play. The combining of the energies is far more important than the results of any effort. We can give someone money, but what we find more important is the process of giving and receiving. In giving someone money, both parties-the giver and the one who receives-have an opportunity to respond relative to the energy of the action. If someone needs money and we feel it important to help and we lend the money they need, is that really helping anyone? Since lending is not giving, we have lost our chance to give because of our fear that we may need our money back.

Most of what has been talked about so far are obvious contrasts. Many of the more interesting contrasts in energy are much more subtle. These subtler contrasts are what makes this plane of existence so beautiful. So let's move from our theoretical black and whites to the grays.

If we look at the trunk of a tree, we may say that is pretty, but if we expand our view to contrast it against its green leaves, it becomes beautiful. If we were to expand our view again and contrast the trunk and leaves against the sky, the tree becomes majestic. The sky by itself is pretty, but with the contrast of the clouds, it also becomes beautiful. Different shades of color have a contrasting affect; each compliments another. These contrasts are not only in color but also help in definition. One tree contrasted against another, one philosophy against another, one religion against another, or one person against another, allows us to derive our definitions. Beauty and understanding come through the relationship established by contrasting one thing or idea against another.

These subtler contrasts come by varying the input of energy from the more major energies. For instance, the color pink contains more light than the color red. By changing the ratio between light and dark, variations appear in religion, philosophy, theology, and science. Varying this relationship between light and dark gives us a specific outcome that can only be discovered when compared to other similar relationships. Without this comparison, we think that ours is the only truth. Truth is always a direct function of where our awareness is focused in any relationship. Truth is the line represented in the Yin-Yang symbol which separates the contrasting energies. The confusion comes from the fact that this line is relative to the observer's awareness. It is within the circle, but its exact location is determined by the observer. Different combinations of light and dark result in different truths. The possibilities are infinite. To find two people who believe exactly the same truth about anything would be very rare indeed.

As mentioned before, the key to discovering truth must be in learning to focus one's awareness. Absolute truth exists when light and dark are equally balanced. All other truths will appear to be real, but they are actually deviations from the absolute truth. The way to balance the two energies is to experience both of them to their fullest extent.

To show this in more detail, let's look at a geometric shape and see if we can draw some analogies. One of the most complex, and yet very symbolic, is the Star of David, also known as the Seal of Solomon, and more commonly called a "six pointed star." Its various meanings throughout history are contained in many different religions and philosophies. There are unlimited meanings derived from its shape, depending on what specific lesson is being taught or the context of its application. It becomes apparent that these many definitions are created by people applying a different focus in order to interpret this symbol.

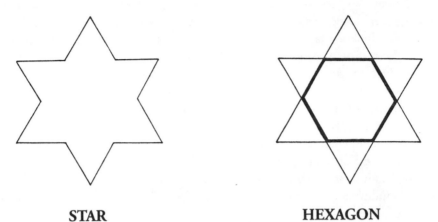

**STAR**                                    **HEXAGON**

Our first instinct, as a function of our normal awareness, is to see the symbol as a star. Stars themselves have many different meanings, but as we shift our awareness, we see that it is really a hexagon surrounded by six triangles (i.e., a very complicated box). However, if we shift our awareness again by adding four lines to the hexagon, the star is completely comprised of triangles. This is not intended to be a study of Pythagorean geometry, but to show that as awareness is shifted, things either become more complex or simpler.

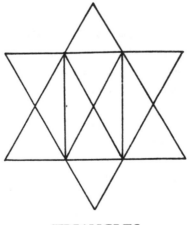

**TRIANGLES**

As we change our focus in order to see all the triangles, it is not the triangles that are interesting per se, but rather their relationship with each other. This particular relationship causes an image of a star to unfold. From this example, we understand that the complex shapes like the star start with a more basic shape. These shapes come together in unique relationships by allowing themselves to multiply and join with themselves to create a new entity. This is used as a fairly common principle in prosperity-type seminars: to be a star, keep repeating a certain action for success.

As a Master, then, we can see a complex picture or symbol and comfortably say that it represents a complicated relationship between simpler things. By altering our focus again, the star becomes two triangles superimposed one on the other. This represents a much simpler relationship, yet a relationship still exists.

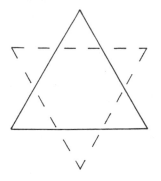

## TWO TRIANGLES

Although the meanings of this symbol are also complex, the Master is able to understand the symbol by breaking it down into simpler forms and relationships. In this case, he would derive the meaning of the two triangles as they superimpose upon themselves pointing in opposite directions to be similar to our yin-yang symbol: a downward movement countered with an upward one.

However, as we look at the triangle, we have uncovered a great mystery, and as we shift our awareness again, we will see how complicated each triangle is. It becomes apparent that although we simplified the star, we have not taken it to its simplest form. Even though we have taken a multisided box and created a three-sided box, don't we still have a box?

We do have one advantage we did not have before; we have a much simpler box to work with. As we shift our awareness to the triangle, the first thing we notice is the relationship that exists between the lines themselves. We see again that it is actually these relationships which create the triangle. If there wasn't a relationship, then the triangle would not exist. So at this point, our awareness tells us that it is not the triangles that comprise the star, but the relationship between the lines.

Being daring, however, we continue and discover that the purpose of the lines is to separate the inner space (the space within the triangle) from the outer space (the space outside the triangle), and, thus, a new relationship is born.

In fact, doesn't the relationship existing between the lines control the relationship of inner space and outer space? This represents an interesting argument: space represents what most of us are trying to achieve: freedom. So what keeps us from merging outer and inner space? The lines. The lines represent definition.

By shifting our awareness, we are primarily trying to simplify definition. Definition is what keeps us from where we want to be-from attaining our sought after goal of freedom.

Now what do we do? We have shifted our awareness enough to allow us to find our real obstacle. If we keep shifting our awareness, can we find a solution? Let's try it.

Since the line seems to be the barrier, let's go inside the line. As we enter into the line, we see a new relationship. The line is comprised of a series of dots, it is not a solid entity as originally thought. It is the relationship of the dots which determines the shape and characteristics of the line. Not only that, but there is space existing between the dots. Isn't that interesting? By shifting our awareness, we found that the space we were seeking is actually an inherent part of what we thought was our obstacle.

However, now we are restricted by the dots from having total freedom. So we go inside the dots (they are just atoms) again with space separating them. If we go into the atom, a new relationship exists-this time between the neutrons, protons, and electrons, and again we find space. In this way, the process continues.

This example is intended to show two principles. The first principle is that by shifting awareness, the relationship that exists between us and the rest of the world becomes clear. Only by changing our awareness can we eventually come close to finding absolute truth. The second point is that only by going into definition (or light, as previously discussed) can we discover space (darkness).

The antithesis of this example could be summed up in the statement that "the answer is always in the question." The searching for an answer (light) is found by shifting awareness into the question (dark). It is reputed that Einstein said, "Every lab assistant has every answer available to him in the universe at his finger tips, he just hasn't asked the right question."

At this point in the shift of our awareness, we have to be really careful not to make erroneous assumptions. For instance, as we break down matter there is more and more space, until a logical assumption would be that space is all there is. But don't forget, we had a choice where to place our awareness. The fallacy in our thinking happened when we went into definition. How would the process have changed if we had seen the star initially as a verb? Couldn't the star itself represent the action of light, independence, and freedom? Seeing the star as an action verb creates an interesting relationship with the dark it is moving through.

Our first example of a star comprised of space and definition represents a horizontal shift in awareness. Horizontal shifts use normal definitions to uncover new relationships. This example of a star being a verb represents a vertical shift in awareness. Vertical shifts require the use of new, different, and sometimes very strange concepts.

Probably as we went through the first example, the thought that "Oh, I understand this" or, "This is fun" prevailed. However, by defining the star as a verb, it probably became very confusing, because the definitions associated with normal thinking no longer apply.

That is why when vertical shifts happen we feel deranged. The world as we see it is no longer the way others see it. The definitions and terminology that apply to normal awareness become outdated and useless as we explore new frontiers.

The challenge of this book is the explanation of the vertical shift I experienced in horizontal shift vocabulary. On the other hand, a vertical shift does not do anyone any good if it can not be brought back to normal awareness levels.

The study of relationships is one of the most important keys to this process of finding freedom-more specifically, the flow of energy that exists within any relationship. This flow of energy can also be symbolized by electricity, and specifically with alternating current. In alternating current, the current alternates between two paths: first it goes in one direction and then in the other.

This is true in all relationships as symbolized by the Yin-Yang symbol. Any energy put into an action will, by nature, eventually reverse direction. If we put our energy into giving, because of its nature, giving has to eventually shift in the other direction causing receiving to happen. The only way this won't happen is if we block off one side, which will automatically shut off the flow of energy. So we see that for every action there is an equal and opposite reaction.

Jesus preached on the importance of activity and, in particular, loving and giving. We see the importance of what He was talking about within the laws of science, where we have applicable specific laws called the "Laws of Momentum." There are basically three laws: when an object is in motion, it will remain in motion unless something stops it; when an object is at rest, it will remain at rest unless something moves it; when an object is in motion, it travels in a straight line unless something interferes with its path. Jesus talked about the importance of activity, because without an impulse of energy, we will stay at rest. In all three laws, the controlling factor is energy, because energy makes us move, stop, or change our direction. However, once the process is started, the momentum of the initial action will keep the process going indefinitely until it is stopped by another impulse of energy.

This implies that if we are experiencing a lack of love, knowledge, money, or health, the situation can only exist for one of two reasons. First, we never created the initial impulse to get it started, we keep stopping it from happening, or something derails it preventing it from its intended target. These are the only three choices.

As we visualize this energy transferring back and forth from one side to the other, I am reminded of a swing in a playground. If we push the swing once, without opposing energies such as friction, the swing will maintain its arc forever. Some people would be content with this movement, but the person interested in mastery would add energy to each side to enlarge the arc. An impetus of activity on one side will make the swing go higher, which in turn gives us more time on the other side. So each time we perform a repetitive action, we want to do a little more by putting a little more energy into it. Granted the ride gets scary when the swing approaches its upper limits, but how else can we ever experience those feelings generated by our activity?

What generally happens in the real world is that we give the swing one push and then watch as it works against normal friction until it comes to a complete stop. Then we may push it again. The friction can be in the form of mixed thoughts counteracting each other; this happens when we are not focused.

Developing a process by which to use this knowledge is rather simple. First we must look at our lives and see the areas where we are unfulfilled. Then we devise an activity around that area which will add an impetus of energy. For instance, if we do not feel loved, we look around at the people in our environment and devise an action to give our love to someone else. Our definition of love is what will be returned to us. If we see love as sex, then sex will be returned. If we see it as a flow of energy, then a flow of energy will be returned. The speed of the return will depend on how much energy we put behind the giving (which we have previously labeled as enthusiasm). Once we give, then we must also be open enough to receive. If we give light (knowledge), then we must be open enough to receive some very fascinating questions.

Discovering the areas where we feel unfulfilled in our lives helps us put together a plan of attack. If we look at these areas and find their opposites, then the purpose of our life will become the activity of giving those things. If we see a lack of love, knowledge, money, or health, then our purpose could be stated as such: I am here to give love, knowledge, prosperity, and health to all the people of the world. The next step would be to then take appropriate action.

By having a purpose derived from action, we can see how the actual games we play become relatively non-important. We see how our present environment (Karma) is comprised of the actions we are currently doing. If we are currently living on the street, it could be because we are comfortable there. If we are a student, it is because we are focusing on our lack of knowledge. And so on.

# Chapter 12

## A Final Note on Freedom

The preceding chapters describe a force that manipulates our lives thereby keeping us in a particular Ring. There are many names for this force: Dharma, Will of God, fate, or destiny. All imply the same meaning with slight differences having a common thread between them that indicates that some force (other than conscious choice) manipulates our lives, taking us through its desired course of action, not ours.

The concept of freedom is contradictory to these concepts. We might respond with the argument that for some people freedom is their destiny. This would be true not for just some people but for all people if we think in terms of ultimate destinies, for all will eventually return to God, which would be freedom. As long as we are pursuing a definite Ring, because of a lack of self-control, we must follow the winds of destiny. Therefore, we are not free. Freedom then can be defined as the state of being beyond destiny, fate, or Dharma, where every action is consciously controlled.

We have also determined that the rings can be classified into two broad categories, which we have called physical or lower level Rings and Mastery or upper level Rings. The difference lies in consciousness: the lower is controlled unconsciously and the upper more consciously. With greater consciousness comes freedom.

We can live our lower Rings by feeling that our lives are controlled by fate and everything that happens is by accident. We can live by Karma believing everything that happens is because of a past deed, by Dharma (pre-destiny), or as some religions teach, because we have sinned or we have entered some sort of spatial or time warp. Whatever reason we choose to give, the results remain the same; we are under the control of someone or something else. Regardless of the theology, this logic strips us of our self-control and, therefore, our opportunity for freedom.

We are faced with three choices when we find the winds of destiny controlling our lives: we can either be happy and sing praises to the source of the winds (praying that we will find a better place to land when the winds let us drop), we can fight, moan, and swear throughout our journey, or we can go outside the winds to the upper Rings and become the directing force of the winds.

It would be relatively simple to move to the logical conclusion that the lower level Rings are really a waste of time and serve no purpose. But if this is truly a recreational planet, then the plan comes into focus because we see everyone pretending not to be God and amusing themselves further by participating in endless games. The other important aspect of these Rings is the opportunity to become a Master of a Ring. Mastership offers us the opportunity to sit back and realize there is much, much more than one particular Ring. It paves the way to the upper Rings and freedom.

The Buddhists have their "Karmic Wheel," which represents a good analogy for a life without change. If we allow the force of destiny to rule our actions, we will remain on this wheel (a never-ending circle) forever. Only by climbing off the wheel can we alter our destiny and find freedom.

Our destiny (or how our lives are planned) allows for no deviation. It is strictly a linear, cause and effect situation. We perform one part of the journey, which leads to the next. Our destiny may keep us entrenched in one Ring, or it may allow for experiences in all four lower Rings. Never does it allow movement into the upper Rings, for movement into these Rings brings the demise of the force controlling our actions. This may lead to great frustration, because although we know deep in our soul that we want to return to God, we are constrained by a life where that is not possible. We are imprisoned within the Karmic Wheel.

Current psychological thought is that this force which imprisons us derives from our subconscious. If we believe Jung, there lies not only our unconscious but the collective unconscious as well. This thought also allows for a possible change in destiny with a change in the subconscious. Because there are enough instances where people have altered their destiny, we can conclude that this is possible. We can also deduce that the way to freedom is accomplished by first changing our destiny. The change in destiny takes us off one wheel of Karma and puts us on another. Being able to create a change implies conscious control, which is the path to freedom.

The Upanishads agree that a change in destiny is possible when it tells us we can change our destiny by changing our actions, which concurs with the importance of the Survival Ring as described herein. It also tells us that just wishing or praying for a change will not in itself create that change, it takes some complimentary form of action, a deed.

We have alluded to this many times throughout this book, but to reiterate, if we want to change our destiny relative to our work, then we must move into the Mental Ring and go to school. The process of returning to school represents a change in our actions and therefore causes a change in our destiny. Aristotle Onasis reportedly once said, "If you want to be rich then you must do the things rich people do." This meant to him that he should move into the rich part of town, join the clubs that the rich frequent, and in general act, as if he were rich. According to the story, this technique is what created his destiny to be the richest man in the world. Unfortunately, many who try this method do it by spending more than they earn, fooling themselves that they are already rich. This, of course, very seldom works because it puts too much pressure on the financial aspect and once inside, they imprisoned further in the never-ending circle of finances. Onasis meant do the actions of the rich, knowing the rich never spend money without some sort of return on their investment.

A problem we encounter in changing our destiny is in the area of missed opportunities. Many times we are afraid to let go of our present situation so that the winds of destiny can move us into the next phase of our lives. Because we hold on so tightly we stay affixed in our comfortable spot. At first the winds blow gentle, but with each opportunity and against a rooted obstacle they blow a little harder. Finally, after several attempts to get us to move, they come at us like a hurricane and totally blast apart our lives leaving those who will not bend lost in a hospital with some stress-related problem. Once freed, however, the winds again gently blow us along the path of our destiny, only now our path might be full of many more obstacles from the destruction caused by the hurricane,

The opposite side is also true for those who try to let go too early. In these cases the winds must blow against us to blow us back to where we need to be. This is easy to decipher when it happens, because we feel the pressure as our new plans don't come to fruition over and over again.

The secret is to wait for the second burst from the winds of change before we let go and as some sages say, wait until the third gust, when it becomes fairly obvious even to the most dense of us that it is time to move. Great examples that tell us it is time to move are when our boss calls us into his office and fires us, our spouse tells us they want a divorce, or the church excommunicates us. All of these are fairly obvious examples of changing winds.

To consciously change our destiny first requires an inherent belief that change is possible. We have all seen changes happen in our lives, where all of a sudden our life course is different. Most often these changes were instituted with the aid of a catalyst: some new person walks into our life or we experience an expected change in our environment. Sometimes, however, they were conscious changes such as we decided to walk away from some apparent opportunity. So most of us do believe that there is a process called change, but we don't know how to tap into it when we need it the most. With the belief that change is possible and the knowledge that a change in our actions will create a change in our destiny, we have an understanding of the whole process.

Of course it is much easier to accept these precepts analytically than to apply them, for we can say we believe, but do we really? Whenever we discount a dream for not being functionally practical or we listen as the world laughs at us for our dreams, we are telling ourselves that we don't believe. If we don't believe, then no amount of action will bring our dream to us, and we will become paranoid and feel the universe is against us.

This is where the practice of meditation comes in. In our meditations, if we can constantly picture ourselves acting as if some particular change has already occurred, while invoking the power of the universe, we will soon become one with the change and ninety percent of the change will already be completed. If done properly, meditation solves two of the obstacles to change: first it reinforces our belief system, and second, it triggers an autonomic response of right action, because our subconscious believes the change has already transpired. All that remains in this formula for change is the other ten percent, which consists of physical action.

One example would be if we wanted to win the lottery. We start by meditating on ourselves already having won the money. We may work years on trying to make that a reality, as we explore our feelings around winning and our actions relative to having so much money all at once. This is the ninety percent. But all this is for naught if we don't ever buy a ticket: the necessary action.

A response to this example might be that we could only win the lottery if it was in our destiny. This is a true statement. If it was part of our destiny, then we would have already won it. The only way anything can happen to us is if it is a part of our destiny.

A better example of change is one that is already in use, the visualization exercises to exorcise cancer from the human body. The people who have participated in these programs meditate and thereby autonomically create change in their lives. They follow nutritional and health guidelines to effect the change they desire in their body: no more cancer. A majority of the people in these programs are able to change their destiny, others are not. If we ask if it is the destiny of those who can't get rid of their cancer to die from their cancer we would have to answer, yes. Then, is it the survivor's destiny to get well using this program? No, it is not. Where we are today is our destiny. Tomorrow, without a change, will present us with yesterday's destiny. The only way change can transpire is with a change in destiny. The people who cure themselves of cancer can only do so by changing their destiny.

The path to freedom takes much work. We can get a sense of the amount of work it takes by reading <u>The Autobiography of a Yogi</u> by Paramahansa Yogananda. He went through a lifetime of discipline with much trial and error, but he reached a point in his life when he could control his destiny at will. Many people may say it was his destiny to become a Master, and it was because he was a Master that he could do all that he did, but I believe that he was a Master because he could control his destiny. When it was time for him to come to the United States, his destiny changed and he became a lecturer. When it was time for him to set up an ashram and an organization to spread his teachings, he became a teacher. When it was time for him to write, he became a writer. Not only did he shift his destiny to become these things, he created them in a way that would allow for great success. Because he was able to do whatever he wished with great success, he was labeled "Master."

This concept is what led Guirdjeff to his conclusion that most of mankind are robots. A robot is totally controlled by an outside force, much like the majority of mankind who are stuck in their Karmic Wheel and controlled by destiny. The only way to become humanized is by first deciphering the chaos presented by human nature into the individual Rings and become aware of our destiny by deciding which is our primary Ring. The process then continues by learning to consciously control our destiny through experiencing the different Rings, followed by movement to the upper Rings as we strive for mastery. With mastery comes our first glimpse of freedom. Once freedom is tasted, the trip back to God is realized.

My wish for you, the reader, is that you choose one area you would like to become successful in and create a change in your destiny that allows for a manifestation of that dream. Do your work today for a better tomorrow and gratefully accept your new life.

# Chapter 13

## Conclusion

Some will say this book is about existentialism, that we are on a path to nowhere, and, therefore, we should learn to enjoy where we are because there isn't any other place to be. Others argue that we have a path which requires us to find freedom by reuniting with God. Both points of view are correct because we are already God. We are just pretending not to be.

Each "Age of Man" has a specific focus within one of the Rings we have discussed in this book. The Piscean Age had its focus within the Christ Realization Ring, as people searched diligently for right definition. The new Aquarian Age has its focus in relationships. This will be a fascinating era, because one can look at relationships in the context of any of the first four Rings.

Even within the human body, there is a relationship between light and dark energies. Generally, Chakra Theory teaches that light energies primarily involve the upper portion of the body and the dark energies involve the lower half of the body. Jesus, because of his adventures into both total light and total darkness, is considered to be the master of both. Throughout religious teachings, many consider the path of Jesus to be through the heart. The heart is the point where the light meets the dark in equal proportions. Only through our heart can absolute truth and detachment be found.

We have redefined the Heart Chakra to contain the energies related to Survival Ring. So this all makes some sense, since the Survival Ring (our physical activities) is the one Ring which sets the earth plane apart from all others. Therefore, all of the concepts previously discussed (unless they can be applied directly in the Survival Ring) really have no value in the process of taking us to freedom. We can derive a fun "Box Theory," but unless it can have practical application in our lives by letting us move with new understanding in new directions, it is just a mental exercise of the Mental Ring level.

Therefore, I deemed it important in each Ring discussed to stress the compensatory actions of the Survival Ring. This is not to criticize the person who wants to play within a specific Ring, that is their choice, but it may lead them to an existential view, because there is no place to go and no way to uncover the absolute truth.

In other religious teachings, there seems to be contradictions to the idea that mastery of the Survival Ring is what we seek. Some teachings refer to the solar plexus as the power point of our bodies, and yet others refer to the Third Eye area. If we examine the teachings of those who refer to the solar plexus, it seems that they are primarily teaching mastery over the worldly things. This Chakra is used because it contains slightly more dark than light. Likewise, those who teach the use of the Third Eye are interested in mastery over spiritual laws and concepts. The Third Eye is comprised of more light than dark. Again, different proportions of light and dark allow for different definitions.

Each approach represents a distinct difference in focus and awareness, and each gives specific and different interpretations to the games we play as well as how we define truth. So all three approaches are correct. In many ways, it is easier to focus our awareness in the solar plexus or Third Eye, rather than in the heart, because the arc of the swing does not have to be as great since it is a little off balance already. If we are not ready for absolutes and the resulting intense chaos, then we should stay away from the path of the heart. All paths are correct paths and will eventually lead to the truth.

We have also seen that at the root of every action is love, and love can be either active or passive. Love is not only the root of all apparent evil, but it is also the root of all apparent good. When we see love in everything, our awareness will automatically shift, and when we learn to respond to everything in our world with unconditional love, both active and passive, we become a Master of all the games. Unconditional love is the art of allowing the swing to move unimpaired, of allowing it to follow its own course.

Normally, we find it relatively easy to criticize someone else's path, or if we don't criticize them, then we feel sorry for them or jealous. I hope this model shows that everyone is playing the game they chose, and we are also playing the game we chose. This philosophy gives us detachment from others and their respective games.

If someone is in their "dead zone," we may cry for them; if someone is reaching for enlightenment, we may lend a hand; but if someone tries to restrict us from attaining freedom, we will fight them. If someone pushes us, we will bend; if someone needs answers, we will give knowledge; if someone has knowledge, we will ask questions; if someone is on the dark path, we will honor it as much as if they were on the light path, because we know it is their choice. Finally, we will not play another's game unless we choose to. All of these are examples of unconditional love.

In the search for spiritual freedom, all that is needed is a shift in awareness. With every horizontal shift comes a certain amount of temporary freedom, but a vertical shift brings total freedom. Horizontal shifts require new definitions, while vertical shifts require non-definition.

Within the ideas outlined in this book, we have reduced the apparent chaos that seemed to exist in our lives to nice little packages which we called Rings, but as we proceeded through our discussion, we found that chaos is important to our growth. We have seen that the swirling chaotic energies are what merges into a point called now, and within this chaos is a still, quiet point where we can see our choices, make our actions, and uncover hidden truths. Therefore, as an initiate, we should be looking forward to the next time chaos comes bursting into our lives.

There is one more point I would like to make about chaos. True chaos is caused by the swirling energies around a vortex, which should be differentiated from the chaos that is caused by non-focus. I am bringing this up because we find that when we are in true chaos, we are neither able to give nor receive because the kinetic energy equals the potential energy. We are fixed in space, unable to move, and at the whim of the rushing currents. To try to grab onto a twig as we rush down the river of life will do nothing but keep us where we are, deep in our chaos.

I am reminded of an analogy that might help to explain some of these concepts. So let me tell you one last story.

## The River

Sweat was pouring off Bill's face in pools of salty water, leaving ridges of white crusts around the corners of his mouth. His clothes were soaked and ragged, yet he continued his trek across the jungle. The denseness of the thicket made his passage feel endless, and it seemed that whenever he finally got to a clearing he could traverse easily, he would find a pride of lions or some other wild beast, forcing him back onto his tedious trail.

Bill was becoming exhausted, not only physically, but mentally as well, because he had to always be on the lookout for snakes, spiders, and other animals which hid in the thicket waiting (or so he thought) for him to come along.

When he first started this trip many years ago , he was excited about the challenge, and he used to save the skins of the animals he killed that were in his way. Now that he was older, he did his best to avoid them.

Bill had originally thought that he could become another Tarzan-like person and tame this jungle, but now it looked like he had become just another jungle animal, except that he was lost. He had lost his bearings many years ago, and if he was ever to find a way out of the jungle, it would be only by the grace of God. (This is the Survival Ring.)

One day as Bill was struggling along, he stumbled upon a river. He was glad to see the water and tore off his shoes to let the water rush between his toes. As he was sitting there on the bank, he thought of a great idea. He logically concluded that rivers always run through towns, and maybe this river could take him out of the jungle, if he would just follow it. (This is the Mental Ring.)

So off he went with his usual thrashing of thicket, as he followed the river upstream. Before long, he realized that there was a better, easier way.

Although he apparently now had a direction for his life, he saw how his life could be made even easier by changing his course of action. (This is the Ethical Ring). Bill reasoned that if he could wade in the water, his path would be easier, so he took off his shoes, rolled up his pant legs, and ventured into the river.

The river was still a pretty difficult path, fighting the current, watching for dangerous fish, snakes, and alligators. His feet were getting cut and bruised on the river bottom, but it was still easier than following the shore path. He also found that if after every twelve steps he beat the water with a stick, he would be a little safer (ritual).

Just as he was getting comfortable with this new path, Bill spied a log floating down the river. He chuckled to himself when he realized that with the shadows falling on it just right, it looked like his mother. Then he became angry, because there was a part of him that felt that his getting lost in the first place was his mother's fault. When he calmed down, he thought, "Wouldn't my life be easier if I grabbed on to something that could help me through this journey? (Freud would love this example of the Conscious Ring.) Bill realized his direction could be changed, but he was glad he had dug his way upstream because it was there he found the log.

After floating alongside the log for awhile, Bill approached a rapid part of the river. He knew if he stayed on the log he would be smashed to bits by the rapids, so Bill very quickly directed the log over to the bank, found a sharp stone, and started whittling himself a canoe. (This is the Precision Ring: the right action at the right time.)

This was a very slow process, but the canoe eventually took form and it wasn't long before he was riding in his canoe down the river. He had finally made a decision that gave him freedom and a much-needed rest. He felt safe in his canoe and his path was smoother. (He was still in his environment, but he had a new box: the Christ-Realized Ring.)

This was great; Bill had a lot of time and a lot more energy. This gave him the opportunity to reflect on his path and on new courses of action. It was during one of his morning swims that Bill put it all together. He had jumped out of his boat and was swimming alongside his canoe, when he really noticed the canoe. His canoe was made of the jungle and yet, it just floated along indifferent to what was happening in the world of the river. It represented a relationship between the jungle and the river. With that thought, Bill laid his head back into the water, pointed his feet downstream, and just floated. As he floated, he felt himself becoming the river (the God-Realized Ring.)

Now that you have read this book, a relationship exists between you and I. The writing of this book has given me the opportunity to give light, love, prosperity, health, and freedom to you. By reading this book, you have participated in this relationship by receiving a flow of energy. This flow has already been started and it can only be stopped by you. It is now your responsibility to give this knowledge, plus more if you wish, to someone else. This, in turn, will allow you to receive even more. Since I have given, I must now open myself up to receive, until the time comes again for me to give more. I love you for participating in this relationship with me.

# References

Author Unknown–1981. <u>Twelve Steps and Twelve Traditions</u>. New York, NY: Alcoholics Anonymous Publishing.

Briggs, J. Peat, F.D.–1984. <u>Looking Glass Universe: The Emerging Science of Wholeness</u>. New York, NY: Simon & Schuster, Inc.

Chopra, D.–1989. <u>Quantum Healing</u>. New York, NY: Bantam Books.

Colton, AR.–1978. <u>Kundalini West</u>. Glendale, CA: Arc Publishing Co.

Becker, R.O., Selden, G.–985. <u>The Body Electric: Electromagnetism and the Foundation of Life</u>. New York, NY: William Morrow and Company.

Emerson, R.W.–1926. <u>Emerson's Essays</u>. New York, NY: Thomas Y. Crowell Co., Inc.

Feng, G., English, J.–1972. <u>Lao-Tzu. Tao Te Ching</u>. New York, NY: Random House.

Globus, Maxwell, Savvidnk.–1976. <u>Consciousness of the Brain</u>. New York, NY: Plenum Press.

Jung, C.G.–1963. <u>Memories, Dreams, Reflections</u>. New York, NY: Vintage Books.

Kirkaldy-Willis, W.H.–1988. <u>Managing Low Back Pain</u>. New York, NY: Churchill Livingston.

Kuhn, T.S.–1970. <u>The Structure of Scientific Revolutions</u>. Chicago, Ill: University of Chicago Press.

Martin, R.J. (ed).–1977. <u>Dynamics of Correction of Abnormal Function: Terrence J. Bennett Lectures</u>. Sierra Madre, CA: Ralph J. Martin, D.C.

Ouspensky, P.D.–1976. <u>In Search of the Miraculous: Fragments of an Unknown Teaching</u>. San Diego, CA: Harcourt Brace Janovich, Publishers.

Palmer, D.D.–1910. <u>The Science, Art, and Philosophy of Chiropractic</u>. Portland, OR: Portland Printing Co.

Selye, H.–1976. The Stress of Life. New York, NY: McGraw-Hill Book Co.

Strachey, J. (ed)–1968. The Standard Edition of the Complete Works of Sigmund Freud. Vol. XX. London : The Hogarth Press.

Ueland, B.–1987. If You Want to Write. St. Paul, MN: Graywolf Press.

Vaughan, F.–1986. The Inward Arc Healing and Wholeness in Psychotherapy and Spirituality. Boston, MA: Shambala.

Wolf, F.A.–1986. The Body Quantum. New York, NY: MacMillan Publishing Co.

# Bibliography

Bach, Richard–1977. Illusions: The Adventures of a Reluctant Messiah. New York, NY: Dell Publishing.

Bly, Robert–1990. Iron John: a Book About Men. Reading, Mass: Addison-Wesley Publishing Co., Inc.

Capra, Fritjof–1975. The Tao of Physics: An Exploration of the Parallels Between Modern Physics and Eastern Mysticism. Boulder, CO: Shambala Publications, Inc.

Castaneda, Carlos–1971. A Separate Reality. New York, NY: Simon and Schuster.

Castaneda, Carlos–1987. The Power of Silence: Further Lessons of Don Juan. New York, NY: Simon and Schuster.

Eiseley, Loren–1969. The Unexpected Universe. New York, NY: Harcourt Brace Jovanovich, Inc.

Gleick, James–1987. Chaos: Making a New Science. New York, NY: Penguin Books.

Harner, Michael–1980. The Way of the Shaman: A Guide to Power and Healing. New York, NY: Bantam Books.

Hoff, Benjamin–1982. The Tao of Pooh. New York, NY: E.P. Dutton, Inc.

Joy, W. Brugh, M.D.–1978. Joy's Way: A Map for the Transformational Journey. Los Angeles, CA: J.P. Tarcher, Inc.

Keen, Sam–1991. Fire in the Belly. New York, NY: Bantam Books.

Kriyananda, Swami–1977. The Path: Autobiography of a Western Yogi. Nevada City, CA: Ananda Publications.

Leadbeater, C.W.–1927. The Chakras. Wheaton, Ill.: The Theosophical Publishing House.

Levine, Stephen–1979. A Gradual Awakening. Garden City, NY: Anchor Books.

Levi–1964. The Aquarian Gospel of Jesus the Christ. Marina Del Ray, CA: Devorss & Co., Publishers.

Ming-Dao, Deng–1983. The Wandering Taoist. San Francisco, CA: Harper & Row, Publishers, Inc.

Moss, Richard–1986. The Black Butterfly: An Invitation to Radical Aliveness. Berkeley, CA: Celestial Arts.

Prather, Hugh–1970. Notes to Myself: My Struggle to Become a Person. New York, NY: Bantam Books.

Satprem–1984. Sri Aurobindo or the Adventure of Consciousness. New York, NY: Institute for Evolutionary Research.

Spalding, Baird T.–1937. The Life and Teachings of the Masters of the Far East. Marina Del Rey, CA: Devorss & Co., Publishers.

Tolstoy, Leo–1984. The Kingdom of God is Within You. Lincoln, NE: University of Nebraska Press.

Woolf, V. Vernon–1990. Holodynamics: How to Develop and Manage Your Personal Power. Tucson, AZ: Harbinger House.

Wright, Robert–1988. Three Scientists and Their Gods: Looking for Meaning in an Age of Information. New York, NY: Harper & Row, Publishers, Inc.

Yogananda, Paramahansa–1974. Autobiography of a Yogi. Los Angeles, CA: Self-Realization Fellowship.

Yogananda, Paramahansa–1975. Man's Eternal Quest and Other Talks. Los Angeles, CA: Self-Realization Fellowship.